香港食家
HONG KONG DINER

JEREMY PANG

CONTRIBUTING AUTHOR
ADRIENNE KATZ KENNEDY

PHOTOGRAPHS BY
KRIS KIRKHAM

quadrille

CONTENTS

INTRODUCTION

In honour and remembrance of my beloved dad, Hiu Ming Pang, who had an undeniable love for Hong Kong, his true home. Also for my son, Theodore Monte Pang: once you are old enough to read, this book will tell you a lot about your Gong Gong, whom you never got to meet, but who spent his life making people smile with food just like this.

Both my parents grew up in Hong Kong; I, however, am what they call BBC – British Born Chinese – which has given me a unique perspective on both cultures. When my parents moved over from Hong Kong to the UK in the 1960s, Chinese food was already well established. In fact, many of the Chinatowns that we know today have barely changed since then. As I have come to learn from my own personal experience, we Chinese are true creatures of comfort. We love our traditions, and hold very close to them, especially in times of change; inadvertently adverse to any significant change in lifestyle. Even within my own city of London, I have met Chinese journalists who, having lived here for many years, have still never been inside many of the little hidden gem shops along the barely three-street-long stretch of the city's Chinatown, instead staying within the comfort of the same old restaurants, just in case the next one isn't quite the same. Creatures of habit indeed!

Although Chinese culture in general may seem to be adverse to immediate change, if I were to pick out what I believe to be the greatest asset to our successful immigration and integration across the world, it is that over time both we and our food are incredibly adaptable. Take the irreplaceable *cha chaan teng* for example: a unique combination both in cuisine and environment of the lasting influence of Western culture in Hong Kong, created as a response to British culture in the 1950s and now held in the hearts of Hong Kongers as a classic example of true Hong Kong cuisine. This is not to be confused with what we consider to be traditional 'Chinese food', with a menu that includes dishes like Macaroni Soup with Spam & Egg (page 78) and Pork Chop Crusty Roll (page 16), not to mention classic Hong Kong Milk Tea (page 156). Never let it be said that Hong Kongers aren't adaptable, because if this isn't a clear example of adaptability then I don't know what is!

Food, to someone with Chinese heritage, is both a source of happiness and a tool which we use to build relationships and trust with others. My own truest and deepest friendships always seem to start over a large table filled with food to be shared.

Hong Kong is famous for its metropolis status: it is home to some of the world's tallest buildings and sky-high restaurants, serving some of the best food out there. The city is constantly in flux, changing, pushing the boundaries of modernity. But I believe that what lies at the heart of this shiny, small, but infinitely layered city is the epitome of Chinese comfort food: the Hong Kong diner. The long reign of casual, café-style and roadside eating is a culture both sustained and fuelled by the 'no-change' attitude I mentioned earlier; providing comfort, happiness and even stability to those nestled in this ever-modernizing Jetson-like city. This seeming juxtaposition of ever-changing and evolving city, continuing to build its towers higher and higher, block by block, but at the same time housing the never-changing street food culture; the same queues wrapped around local favourites, bypassing the trendy for the steadfast staples decade upon decade – from peanut butter French toast, used to mop up lashings of condensed milk, to a bowl of beef brisket noodle soup at any time of the day – this is the real beating heart of this fair city. In my view, Hong Kong diner food should be considered some of the best of world cuisine. From the fresh ingredients to the care with which they are used, to the comforting, flavourful, straightforward, unpretentious, interactive way in which they are served, I cannot help but think of my numerous experiences eating in Hong Kong diners without feeling as though I have been engulfed and enriched alongside being well fed. Despite such places becoming more and more buried beneath the concrete jungle, I hope that true 'Hong Kongers' out there will agree that their diner-style eating habits, in whatever form, will never be swallowed up completely by big buildings with fancy restaurants on top.

There are many different types of Hong Kong diner worth mentioning, each with their own style of cooking and varying menu sizes. Equally, each different style of diner also highlights a particular skill or technique that I find nothing short of astounding. From the *dim sum* chef to the man with his paper-thin wok on the side of the road, each hones a very specialized skill which I hope to, one day, find enough time and dedication to acquire. I hope that as you read this book not only will you try some of the recipes I've researched and created, but also you will become equally excited and curious by the snippets of history of the city's unique eateries that I have included, along with some of my experiences, which have endeared this city to me, and inspired my cooking.

To many, Chinese cooking has always been a well-kept secret among those in the know. However, what many may not realize is that Chinese food, especially Cantonese food, most famously from Hong Kong and its surrounding region of South China, has been heavily influenced by the Western world. Even the specialist breads from the local bakeries bear a considerable resemblance to the French brioche, just with the addition of spam, barbecued pork or coconut custard on the inside or a good old British crumble on top instead! Hong Kong, once named the 'Pearl of the Orient', has had its fair share of Western occupation and influence. And when it comes to cultural invasion, interaction or occupation, no matter what part of the world it comes from, you can always trace back the history by means of the trail of food left behind.

With years of being a huge 'commuter town' from East to West, it comes as no surprise that Hong Kong has such a diverse, on-the-move culture and dining scene. From *cha chaan tengs* (tea house lounges), to *dai pai dongs* (street hawker stalls), *dim sum* houses with their moving trolleys of hot pick-up-and-stuff-your-face style dumplings, and one-dish specialist cafés, to the unique dessert houses and bakeries that line the city's streets and hidden alleys, each one is able to tell one small but distinct portion of Hong Kong's unique story.

After seeking out and trying many wonderful examples of each of these distinct types of street-style eatery, then standing back to marvel at how they all interweave and overlap with each other, it is no wonder that this culture and city serve as such an inspiration for me, and for what I try to bring to my own cooking: playfulness, simplicity, a sense of family and community and a nod to my own family's history, all set against the backdrop of a cosmopolitan, diverse, historical and ever-changing community. This is the food I love to cook because this is the food I love to eat.

EXPERIENCING HONG KONG FOOD CULTURE
UP CLOSE AND PERSONAL

I've been travelling back and forth to Hong Kong since a young age, and although my most recent trip there was originally vaguely planned around my memories and eating experience as a ravenous teenager and beyond, this time around the pressure was on, as we had planned for at least three different groups of friends to be out there, all specifically for the hard task of eating our way around the city. Luckily, no particular dietary requirements were sent to me in advance – everyone arrived in Hong Kong at different times with an open food mind, and I knew that my business partners Nev and Max would be on hand to eat whatever was left on the table if the others weren't up to the task. Adrienne, as contributing author of the book, had the sole job of tasting everything that was put in front of her and had to take note of anything that might inspire the recipes (outside of just my head), so she had to work out quite quickly how to pace herself through the Hong Kong tour.

HERE'S ADRIENNE'S EXPERIENCE OF WHAT IT TAKES TO EAT LIKE A HONG KONGER

Having spent years learning about Chinese cuisine and its culture through work with Jeremy and School of Wok, I felt in a broad sense that I had come to possess a certain level of understanding and knowledge about the subject matter. But let it be said that nothing, NOTHING, can serve as a substitute for the real thing. Google and books are a great start, but can only take you so far. Since returning from Hong Kong I have been humbly reminded of the value of first-hand knowledge: taking in the sights and sounds, the atmosphere, and the flavours alongside the people who cook, create and serve, as well as those who eat and enjoy.

In the creating of this book a two-week, packed-to-the-brim, whirlwind, food-engorged, sensory-overloaded research trip to Hong Kong was both planned and led by Jeremy himself. A trip consisting of no less than eight meals a day, and a tour guide, both of which have since been infamously and lovingly dubbed #Pangtours by the merry band of men and women, growing in both number and waist size as the days went on. Jeremy, despite his stature, is the speediest of walkers, with boundless energy matched only by that of a two-year-old hyped up on candyfloss.

During our Hong Kong trip we were lucky enough to visit a wide variety of eateries: from tiny specialist cafés serving only a few well-made dishes, to street-side *dai pai dongs*; from entirely outdoor restaurants set up on unannounced roadside alleys, to 1950s style *cha chaang tengs* or tea house lounges, lined with gleaming sheets of Formica, towers of condensed milk tins for making copious amounts of strong milk tea, and some with the very first owner, pushing ninety, still working the till. Each eatery was equally captivating and inspiring but for very distinct reasons, none of which was a lengthy menu, a slick interior or a state-of-the-art anything.

Delving into Hong Kong cuisine and culture, I found it illuminating how each twisted around the other, making it difficult to tell which came first. The more days we spent following Jeremy on his expertly curated food tour, the more steps we took, the more samples we tried, the more cultural customs we began to understand and use; from how to order, to what order to eat things in, to the customary practice of washing our own bowls and spoons table-side. We began to pick up clues on how to distinguish the hidden gems (of which there are many) from the tourist traps (of which there are also many). The more information we gathered, the richer the experience became, and the more endearing the city, its quirky yet resourceful people and its abundance of truly spectacular dishes had become to each one of us. Why Hong Kong is not more well known internationally for its local eateries is beyond me, because they are far richer, more captivating, more spectacular and more revealing of true Hong Kong culture than any flashing skyscraper on its magnificent skyline.

Refer to our guide (at the back of the book) to help you retrace our footsteps on our whirlwind trip into discovering the intriguing gems of Hong Kong eating for when you next visit.

TIPS & TRICKS OF HONG KONG STYLE COOKING

Hong Kong is one of the most densely populated cities in the world, so cooking, whether at home or as a chef on the streetsides of the city, must be done with efficiency in mind. This is a city where apartment sizes are likened to the size of large parking spaces, where space is limited, and home kitchens are often a secondary thought, or else there would be nowhere to sleep. Limited space in kitchens means that there are no ovens; sometimes fridges and freezers are hard to fit into the tiny kitchens, so Hong Kongers find themselves either eating out more if they can afford to, or going to the market on a daily basis to save space and still be able to cook fresh food. Despite first appearances, the lack of space also lends itself to some clear positives: Hong Kong cooks and chefs have an amazing sense of resourcefulness when it comes to cooking. Every single surface in the kitchens or streetside tables is used to prep or cook, stacking ingredients, prepped or not, on top of each other, using height, not length, to make more room. So long as there is space for a wok, cleaver, chopping board, and possibly a steam basket stored on top of the wok, you can make a banquet worth bragging about.

Here are some general tips and tricks that I have picked up from Hong Kong chefs. Their tiny kitchen layouts, efficient use of each part of every ingredient or leftover, and quick, high-heat cooking that seals flavour into the ingredients within minutes are all noteworthy skills well worth mastering in order to create a true Hong Kong kitchen.

COOK ONCE EAT TWICE

Saving food from an ethical point of view may not be a clear-cut direct message for Hong Kong people, but it is ingrained in Chinese culture that we must never waste, and that every food that can be eaten, must be eaten. This book is an attempt to create more fun and learning in the kitchen, but I also hope it serves as a good and honest representation of how Hong Kong people like to eat, and how we value our food. My wife, Dee, often wonders how I manage to bring out a meal from what appears to be an empty fridge, but the real trick is that we always have a very full freezer, and an even more full pantry with good Tupperware at the ready! Therefore it's no magic trick to make another meal out of good home-cooked leftover dishes and a few dry, fermented or saucy ingredients – it simply requires a bit of resourcefulness coupled with a dash of creativity.

Any of the dumplings, *baos* and sharing dishes from this book are likely to present you with leftovers (unless you really are a big eater). So don't hesitate to utilize your freezer to make numerous meals for the rest of the week, or even a whole table full of banquet or party food when your friends come over next. Remember, true Chinese-style eating is all about having a variety of foods on the table; the little bits and bobs can really add up to a memorable and satisfying meal, saving you room in the waste bin and hard-earned cash as well.

DOUBLE FRYING & DOUBLE COOKING

Much like all other Chinese cuisines, stir-frying, steaming and deep-frying formulate the basis of Hong Kong cuisine, in addition to our love of roast meats. Pre-blanching of meats or vegetables, whether in hot oil or hot water, speeds up the cooking process by creating an immediate seal around whatever ingredient is being cooked. This initial seal and 'first cook' not only keeps the meat or vegetables nice and tender, but it also caramelizes any natural sugars around the edges of the meat if fried, and brings out any fatty impurities if blanched in water. It is also a less 'faffy' way of sealing every side of the meat in a frying pan, which requires having to turn every piece over time and time again to get the same effect. Once placed back in the wok the second time round to finish off a dish, the ingredients will then soak up the sauce for a stir-fry, with more of a caramelized finesse. This double cooking technique in Chinese cuisine is also used as a tool to speed up the finishing of dishes. For example: if you blanch sliced asparagus, green beans or broccoli for 1–2 minutes in advance, then cool them immediately in cold water, the vegetables will cook much quicker when flash-fried into a steaming hot sauce later on, enabling you to turn a stir-fried vegetable dish out in seconds rather than minutes, while maintaining a fresh and natural crunch.

When blanching anything during the double cooking process, a wok mesh strainer will help to do the job in one swift swoop. I call these tools 'spiders': they are essentially giant flat sieves with a large web-like metal mesh surface and a bamboo handle, which allow you to pick up a wokful of ingredients in one go.

Double cooking does not have to be unique to Chinese cooking. Once you get used to the benefits of cooking this way, it's a great cooking technique that can be used either to speed up the cooking process, crisp up or seal whatever you are cooking, enabling you to move on to the next step quicker and more efficiently.

THE WOK CLOCK

Repetition is definitely not in my eating nature, as I'm the type of person who must eat a different meal each day of the week or else get bored. However, when it comes to cooking and teaching, I find that repetition of simple learning techniques helps a lot. Since writing *Chinese Unchopped*, the Wok Clock has proved a popular tool for preparation and organization and keeps the cooking in mind at all times, as opposed to losing track by re-reading the recipe over and over again. And when it comes to cooking in small spaces, much like in Hong Kong street stalls, organization of your prep is by far the best way to keep your kitchen tidy.

At School of Wok, we like to prepare our ingredients in an organized manner, using a round plate as a clock that Nev, my business partner, and I like to call the Wok Clock. This organization is not exclusive to wok cooking, but 'Wok Clock' is just a simple phrase to remember and should help with organizing all types of cooking at home. Once you have prepared all your ingredients, start to place them in their cooking order, beginning at 12 o'clock, working your way all around the plate. Whether you are cooking a stir-fry or a slow-cooked curry, it works. As a general rule of thumb we tend to start with the base ingredients (onions, garlic, ginger) and firmer vegetables, then move on to the meats or other proteins, followed by the sauce or braising liquid. It's that simple! I remind you to use this Wok Clock method many times throughout the book. Once you get into the habit of doing so, you'll find cooking as a whole to be a much neater and more straightforward process, freeing you up to relish the joys of preparing dishes and learning new techniques rather than scampering to consult your recipe books.

USING BASE SAUCES, SIDES & EXTRAS

You will find throughout the book that there are various recipes that use base sauces: either directly from the pantry, ones which use additional chilli sauces or oils to be used as condiments, or in conjunction with other fresh ingredients to create a completely new recipe. Getting your head around Chinese sauces can be quite daunting, but the easiest way to explain them is to see the sauces as vehicles that help to accentuate the natural flavour of the raw ingredients you are cooking. Chinese sauces and condiments are usually quite powerful in flavour. As a general rule of thumb they are there either to sit on the side for added flavour, or within sauces and marinades to accentuate depth of flavour from natural ingredients, whichever part of your palate you are trying to hit.

For example, Chiu Chow chilli oil (whether homemade or not), is a strong, spicy-flavoured condiment. Just a quarter or half a teaspoon, mixed with some light soy sauce, oyster sauce, a little pinch of sugar and some chicken stock, will lighten the spice. And while the mild essence of chilli could help to cut through something as delicate as a scallop, or help to balance out the meatiness of a dumpling, it is unlikely to 'burn' your delicate tastebuds, even if chilli is not your usual go-to ingredient. Balance is key!

Throughout the book, you will find different uses of base sauces and condiments, and you may find it interesting to experiment with tweaking recipes here and there once you have gained the confidence from cooking the recipes once or twice. The ability to switch and change sauces is where Hong Kong diner chefs really work their magic. In a Hong Kong street kitchen, all the sauces will be lined up right next to the wok burners, next to the salt, sugar, white pepper and other condiments, for the chefs to pick out small quantities with the tips of their wok ladles as they are cooking. Part of the fun of cooking is in the experimentation, so don't be afraid to play around!

街頭小食
STREET SNACKS

豬扒脆皮包

PORK CHOP CRUSTY ROLL

HONG KONGERS LOVE ALL THINGS PORK. Pork offal, porky snacks, roasted pork *bao*, braised pork, sweet and sour pork … YOU NAME IT, WE CAN COOK IT. These fried pork chop buns, with the chop bone kept in to stay true to Hong Kong style eating, will make you salivate throughout the whole cooking process. Whether served in a cheap crusty roll, a soft bap or a homemade pineapple bun (see page 159), the crisp outer edges and succulent meat of the pork chop are GUARANTEED TO MAKE YOUR MOUTH WATER.

SERVES 2

2 pork chops, on the bone
    (approx. 200–250g/7–9oz each)
2 crusty rolls of your choice
vegetable oil, for frying
1 tomato
4 leaves of lettuce – baby gem
    or iceberg recommended for a
    good crunch
Japanese mayonnaise (you can find
    this in many Asian supermarkets)

THE MARINADE
½ teaspoon sugar
¼ teaspoon salt
¼ teaspoon white pepper
1 clove of garlic
a pinch of five-spice
1 tablespoon Shaoxing rice wine
1 tablespoon light soy sauce
2 tablespoons cornflour (cornstarch)

Keeping the meat on the bone, slice into the edges of each pork chop 3 or 4 times, creating slits all the way through that will help keep the meat flat when cooked. Then, turn your knife or cleaver upside down and, using the blunt end, bash the meat as many times as possible to flatten it out, making tracks along the pork. This will begin to tenderize the chop and allow the marinade to soak into the meat well.

Once flattened, a similar thickness to an escalope, mix the marinade ingredients together and massage into the chops until they are completely coated. Leave in the fridge, ideally overnight, and for a minimum of 1 hour, to marinate.

Slice the crusty rolls in half, ready for the fried pork chops. Cut the tomato into thin slices, and make sure your lettuce is washed and patted dry so it maintains its crunch.

Traditionally in Hong Kong, the chops are deep-fried to order. Half-fill a wok or deep-fryer with vegetable oil and heat to 180°C (350°F), or use a wooden skewer or wooden chopstick to test by placing the tip in the oil: if the wood starts to fizz after a second or so, the oil is hot enough. Deep-fry the chops for 5 minutes (turning once), until golden brown, then place on a few sheets of kitchen paper to drain off any excess oil.

You can also shallow-fry the chops. Pour roughly 5mm (¼ inch) of oil into a large frying pan, bring to a medium-high heat, then place the chops in the frying pan one by one. Fry for 2–3 minutes on each side, until golden brown all over, then place on a few sheets of kitchen paper to drain off any excess oil.

Once the chops are done, put them directly into the crusty rolls, followed by a couple of slices of tomato and some lettuce. Squeeze a dollop of Japanese mayonnaise over the top, put the crusty top on the roll, and serve.

煎釀豆腐

FRIED STUFFED TOFU

SERVES 4

1 block of firm fresh tofu
cornflour (cornstarch), for dusting
vegetable oil, for frying

THE FILLING
1 clove of garlic
2 sprigs of fresh coriander (cilantro)
1 spring onion (scallion)
100g (3½oz) skinless dace fillet
  (swapsies: coley fillet)
¼ teaspoon salt
¼ teaspoon cracked black pepper
¼ teaspoon sugar
1 teaspoon pure sesame oil
½ tablespoon cornflour (cornstarch)

DIPPING SAUCES
3 tablespoons hoisin sauce, mixed
  with 1 tablespoon water
2 tablespoons sriracha chilli sauce

Finely chop the garlic, coriander (cilantro) and spring onion (scallion). Put the fish fillet, chopped garlic, salt, pepper, sugar, sesame oil and cornflour (cornstarch) into a food processor and blitz well until a smooth paste is formed. Once blitzed, mix in the spring onion and coriander.

Slice the tofu into 3cm (1¼ inch) squares, roughly 1cm (½ inch) thick. Use a teaspoon to spoon out the inside of each square, to make a 'crater' in each square of tofu. Lightly dust each crater and the top edges of the tofu with ⅓ teaspoon of cornflour to help stick the filling to the tofu. Take roughly 2 teaspoons of filling and spread it carefully into each crater and generously over the top of the tofu squares. Repeat until either the filling is finished or there are no more tofu squares left to fill.

Bring a frying pan to a medium-high heat, and cover the base with approximately 2 tablespoons of vegetable oil. Once the oil is hot, pan-fry the tofu pieces carefully, fish side first. Fry for 3–4 minutes, until golden brown, then flip the pieces over and fry for a further 3 minutes.

Serve as a snack or starter, with the thinned-down hoisin sauce and sriracha chilli sauce for dipping.

TIP: IF YOU DON'T FINISH ALL THE FILLING, YOU CAN USE THE REST TO MAKE SIMPLE FISH CAKES FOR A SNACK OR STARTER. JUST ROLL IT INTO SMALL FISH BALLS, FLATTEN AND PAN-FRY.

特脆韭菜卷

DOUBLE-SIDED CRISPY CHIVE ROLL

Wrapping these OVERSIZED STREET-STYLE ROLLS is very simple, much like wrapping up a present. SHANGHAI DUMPLING PASTRIES can be found in most Chinese supermarkets, either fresh or frozen. They are slightly larger than wonton pastries, which is why they make a GREAT PROPER-SIZED SNACK.

SERVES 4–5

30 Shanghai dumpling pastries
3 tablespoons vegetable oil

THE FILLING
1 clove of garlic
½ a thumb-size piece of ginger, peeled
2 spring onions (scallions)
300g (10½oz) Chinese chives
100g (3½oz) green cabbage
100g (3½oz) minced pork

THE MARINADE
½ tablespoon oyster sauce
1 tablespoon light soy sauce
1 teaspoon pure sesame oil
½ teaspoon sugar

TO SERVE
10 bamboo skewers
2:1 ratio of light soy sauce and Chinese rice vinegar, for dipping

Mix the marinade ingredients together in a small bowl. Finely chop the garlic, ginger, spring onions (scallions), Chinese chives and cabbage and place in a mixing bowl. Add the minced pork, then massage the marinade well into the mixture.

Take a dumpling pastry and place it straight in front of you. Place roughly 1½ teaspoons of the marinated pork mix in the centre of the pastry. Fold in half, bringing the bottom half of the pastry over the top of the filling to meet the top edge of the pastry. Dab a little water over the top of the pastry and roll the filling portion over, to stick much like a sausage roll. Next, dab some water on the pastry 'wings' on both sides of the filling. Firmly fold one wing to the centre, then fold the second wing over the top of the first to overlap, sticking it down securely.

Repeat until either all the pastries or all the filling have been used up.

Heat the vegetable oil to a medium-high heat in a large frying pan. Place the pastries in the oil and flip them over straight away; this ensures that you do not need to add much more oil and prevents the pastries from getting too greasy. Pour 3 tablespoons of water over the top of them and quickly cover with a lid, repeating this process once every minute for roughly 3–4 minutes, or until the bases are golden brown. This will steam and fry your dumplings simultaneously.

Flip them once more and fry the other side in exactly the same way, intermittently adding a little water, then covering with a lid to steam them through. When both sides are golden brown, remove the lid and fry for 1 minute further on each side, to allow the pastries to crisp up once again.

Serve on skewers, with a mixture of soy sauce and vinegar on the side, for dipping.

港式咖哩魚蛋

HONG KONG CLASSIC CURRIED FISH BALLS

This is one of those FAMOUS STREET FOOD DISHES that Hong Kong is known for. Though it may seem like an odd combination for a street food dish to those who have not spent much time in Asia before, they are a staple and can be found ABSOLUTELY EVERYWHERE across the city. You can't visit a market or busy shopping centre without seeing a stand selling these, normally with a crowd around the stall of both locals and tourists alike, tucking into skewers of FRESHLY MADE FISH BALLS. Whether cooked in the curry sauce or with the sauce kept on the side for dipping, this slightly 'upscale' version is a MUCH-LOVED HONG KONG CLASSIC.

TIP: THE FISH BALLS CAN ALSO BE DEEP-FRIED. HALF-FILL A WOK OR DEEP-FRYER WITH VEGETABLE OIL AND HEAT TO 180°C (350°F), OR USE A WOODEN SKEWER OR WOODEN CHOPSTICK TO TEST THE OIL BY PLACING THE TIP IN THE OIL: IF THE WOOD STARTS TO FIZZ AFTER A SECOND OR SO, THE OIL IS HOT ENOUGH. DEEP-FRY THE FISH BALLS FOR 3 MINUTES, UNTIL GOLDEN BROWN. DRAIN ON KITCHEN PAPER FOR A MINUTE OR SO BEFORE SERVING.

TIP: IF YOU ARE KEEN TO DIP YOUR TOE IN FIRST, YOU CAN START BY TRYING READY-MADE FISH BALLS WITH THE CURRY SAUCE, AS THERE ARE MANY TYPES AVAILABLE IN CHINESE SUPERMARKETS. TAKE YOUR PICK, THEN JUST MAKE THE CURRY SAUCE AND HEAT UP THE SHOP-BOUGHT TREATS.

SERVES 3–4

**THE FISH BALL MIX
(MAKES 25–30 FISH BALLS)**
400g (14oz) skinless, boneless Spanish mackerel fillets (swapsies: monkfish cheeks)
100g (3½oz/¾ cup) raw, peeled and deveined prawns (shrimp)
1 teaspoon sea salt
¼ teaspoon ground white pepper
1 teaspoon sugar
1 teaspoon pure sesame oil
1 egg white
2 teaspoons cornflour (cornstarch)
1 teaspoon fish sauce
20ml (¾fl oz) water

THE CURRY SAUCE
2 cloves of garlic
2 large fresh red chillies
10 fresh curry leaves
3 tablespoons vegetable oil
100g (3½oz/1 cup) finely diced onion
500ml (18fl oz/2 cups) chicken stock
1 tablespoon fish sauce
1 tablespoon cornflour (cornstarch), mixed with 3 tablespoons water

THE CURRY PASTE
1 tablespoon Madras curry powder
¼ teaspoon chilli powder
1 tablespoon light soy sauce
¼ teaspoon salt
1 teaspoon sugar
3 tablespoons coconut milk

For best results, use an electric mixer with the k-mixer attachment. If you don't have a mixer, you can use a food processor.

Slice the fish into small pieces, and bash the prawns (shrimp) with a cleaver. Put both into the mixer. Start the mixer on a low speed and mix well for 1–2 minutes. Then add the rest of the fish ball mix ingredients and turn the speed up to medium. Once all the ingredients are well mixed, turn up to high for 2 minutes, until a smooth paste has formed.

To make the fish balls, bring a large saucepan, three-quarters filled with water, to the boil. Have a small bowl of cold water nearby. Dip your hands into the cold water, then make one ball at a time with the fish mixture and drop them straight into the boiling water as they are made. Once the fish balls float to the top of the water, they are ready either to cool, freeze and reheat another time, or to set aside for later in the recipe.

To make the curry sauce, finely chop the garlic, red chillies and onions and pick the fresh curry leaves. Mix together all of the curry paste ingredients until they form a smooth paste. **Now build your wok clock:** place the garlic at 12 o'clock, followed by the red chilli, curry leaves, curry paste and lastly the chicken stock.

You are now ready to make your curry sauce. Pour the vegetable oil into a medium saucepan and bring to a medium heat. Fry the onion for roughly 5–6 minutes, stirring occasionally, until well softened and starting to brown. Add the garlic, red chilli and curry leaves and continue to fry for another 2–3 minutes. After about 30 seconds, you should start to smell the distinct aroma of the curry leaves. Do not allow the leaves to burn, but once they are starting to brown a little, add the curry paste and stir well. It should start to boil within about 30 seconds or so. Continue to stir the paste for 2–3 minutes, until it is just about sticking to the base of the pan. At this point, pour in a quarter of the chicken stock and bring to the boil once more.

Once the sauce has reduced by half, pour the rest of the stock into the pan and bring to the boil. Then bring the heat down to a simmer and continue to cook for 30 minutes, or until reduced by half again, keeping the saucepan uncovered. Season the sauce to taste with fish sauce (this is used for saltiness and will complement the fish balls).

Once the sauce has been reduced, add 1 tablespoon of the cornflour paste and stir, while boiling, to thicken it slightly.

Finally, either reheat the fish balls in boiling water for 3–4 minutes, or add them to the curry sauce for 5–10 minutes to reheat and soak up the sauce. Serve with bamboo skewers on the side for a great treat or snack.

豬腸粉

MARKET STYLE CHEUNG FUN

Traditionally, a RECTANGULAR STEAMER is used to make *cheung fun*. If you have access to a specialist *cheung fun* steamer, great, but if not, you can also make it in a LARGE ROUND SAUCEPAN that has a stainless steel steamer tray and lid that sit on top of the pan. At home, I actually use a small oven gastronome tray to hold the water, with the same size of steam tray placed over the top, then a larger flat tray as the lid for the steamer, to allow myself more ROOM TO MANOEUVRE when making the rice rolls.

SERVES 2–3 ALONGSIDE OTHER DIM SUM OR SIDE DISHES

THE *CHEUNG FUN* BATTER
250g (9oz/1¾ cups) rice flour
70g (2½oz/½ cup) tapioca starch
35g (1¼oz/⅓ cup) cornflour
  (cornstarch)
900ml (1½ pints/just under 4 cups)
  water
50ml (2fl oz) vegetable oil
½ teaspoons salt
vegetable oil, for brushing

THE SWEETENED SOY SAUCE
3 tablespoons light soy sauce
1 teaspoon sugar
3 tablespoons hot water

THE CONDIMENTS
toasted sesame seeds
sesame paste
hoisin sauce
Chiu Chow chilli oil

Put all the *cheung fun* batter ingredients, apart from the oil, into a large mixing bowl and whisk well until smooth and even, then add the vegetable oil and mix once more. The batter will seem very watery, but don't worry. Cover and put into the fridge for 30 minutes.

Meanwhile, mix the sweetened soy sauce ingredients together in a small jug or bowl.

Fill a saucepan or the base of the steamer, whatever you choose to use, halfway up with boiling water. Lightly brush the steamer tray with oil, then line it with greaseproof paper, spreading it as flat as possible, much like lining a cake tin. Brush the top of the greaseproof generously with more oil.

Once the steamer is set up, take the batter out of the fridge. Before using it, stir well 5 or 6 times from the bottom of the bowl to ensure that all the flour is incorporated into the mix.

Place the steamer tray over the pan of hot water and bring the water to the boil on a high heat. Once steaming hot, pour 1–1½ ladles of batter on to the greaseproof paper and allow it to heat up. It will seem like nothing is happening for the first minute or so, but very quickly you will see the batter starting to solidify and become more jelly-like. At this point, if there are any pockets that have little or no batter, fill them up with a drop or two of extra batter.

Then cover the steamer tray with a lid and steam for exactly 3 minutes.

Now remove the lid. You should see the batter bubbling up off the greaseproof paper in places. The *cheung fun* is now cooked. Reduce the heat under the pan or steamer to low, then very carefully pick up the whole sheet of greaseproof paper and place it on a clean surface. Using the greaseproof to help you, roll the *cheung fun* up, like a mini Swiss roll, and slide it on to a plate.

To serve, cut into bite-sized portions. Brush with a little oil, scatter toasted sesame seeds over the top, then pour over the sweetened soy sauce mix. Have the rest of the condiments ready on the side, ready to dip the pieces of rice roll into for pure Hong Kong breakfast pleasure.

MARBLED TEA EGGS

MAKES 12

60g (2¼oz/¼ cup) salt
12 fresh eggs, at room temperature

THE MARBLING MARINADE
2 star anise
1 small cinnamon stick
zest of 1 tangerine
3 tablespoons jasmine tea leaves
½ teaspoon salt
½ a thumb-size piece of ginger
4 spring onions (scallions)
2 tablespoons light soy sauce
6 tablespoons dark soy sauce
1 litre (1¾ pints/4 cups) water

Put all the marbling marinade ingredients into a small saucepan and bring to the boil, then boil for 10 minutes to deepen the colour and steep the tea. Set aside and allow to cool to room temperature, then cover and place in the fridge to chill.

Pour 2 litres (3½ pints/8½ cups) of water into a separate large saucepan, add the salt and bring to the boil. Lower the heat to medium and carefully add the 12 eggs to the pan. Boil for 5 minutes exactly.

Once boiled, place the eggs in a bowl of cold water to cool, running cold water from the tap over them for a minute or so, to ensure that they stop cooking. Once cooled, crack the eggs all the way around the shell, **but do not peel the eggs at this point.**

Once cracked, place the eggs in the chilled marbling marinade for a minimum of 5 hours, or overnight in the fridge. Then peel and serve as a snack with crisps or as a side dish. This is a great accompaniment to a cold beer – Hong Kong style!

釀辣椒茄子串

STUFFED CHILLIES & AUBERGINE STICKS

This snack will transport you straight to the STREETS OF MONG KOK. It is typically consumed in quick succession with several other street food dishes, all while walking along the BUSY MARKET STREETS, where the neon lights are guaranteed to keep you awake no matter how full you are or what time of day it is. When made at home, this type of snack splits the difference between HEALTHY AND INDULGENT, and makes great party food too.

SERVES 4

10 large fresh green chillies
2 Chinese aubergines (eggplants)
50g cornflour (cornstarch)
vegetable oil, for frying

THE FILLING

½ a spring onion (scallion)
100g (3½oz/¾ cup) raw, peeled and deveined prawns (shrimp)
100g (3½oz) skinless cod fillet (swapsies: any white fish fillet)
100g (3½oz) cleaned squid tubes
¼ teaspoon salt
a pinch of white pepper
1 teaspoon pure sesame oil
1 tablespoon cornflour (cornstarch)

THE CONDIMENTS

1 tablespoon sweet soy sauce (kecap manis)
3 tablespoons hoisin sauce
3 tablespoons sriracha chilli sauce

Slice the green chillies in half and remove the seeds, keeping the chilli halves intact. Slice the aubergines (eggplants) into 3–4cm (1¼–1½ inch) rounds, then carefully scoop out most of the centre of the aubergine pieces, cutting a rough cone shape while leaving a thin layer of flesh still at the base to keep the filling from leaking out, creating aubergine 'shot glasses' that can be filled with the mix. Spooning out half the aubergine flesh will allow space for the fish filling.

Finely chop the spring onion (scallion) and set aside. Put the rest of the filling ingredients into a food processor and blitz on a high speed, until a smooth paste has formed. Open the processor and run a fork through the mix, to check for any large lumps of seafood or fish. Blitz once more for good measure, until completely smooth. Once smooth, add the chopped spring onion to the mix and fold in with a spatula or spoon.

Lightly dust the inside of the chillies and aubergines with cornflour (cornstarch). Then spoon in the filling until it is flush to the edge of the vegetables.

Traditionally these snacks are deep-fried; however, for home cooking, shallow-frying the stuffed veg will make them just as tasty and less oily.

Fill a large frying pan with enough oil to shallow-fry the vegetables (roughly 5mm/¼ inch). Bring the oil to a medium heat and wait until you can feel the heat by holding your hand 5cm (2 inches) above it. Carefully lay the stuffed vegetables in the pan, fish side down, and fry for 4–5 minutes, until the fish mix is golden brown. Use a large spoon to baste each piece well with the hot oil. Once the fish mix has turned a golden brown, turn over and continue to fry the vegetables for a further 3–4 minutes, then add 4 tablespoons of hot water, cover the pan with a lid, and cook for a further 4–5 minutes. Once the vegetables are piping hot all the way through, remove the lid and allow to fry for a further 30 seconds. Place on a couple of sheets of kitchen paper to drain any excess oil.

Serve hot, with a good squeeze of sweet soy sauce drizzled over the top and some hoisin and chilli sauce on the side.

黎建彰潮州蠔餅

ANDY LAI'S CHIU CHOW OYSTER CAKE

Andy Lai works as a CHEF AND ORGANIZER at the Taste Library in Hong Kong; a not-for-profit organization that encourages the community to use their cookbook library, take a free classes or engage in SOCIAL GATHERINGS. The oyster cake recipe itself comes from Chiu Chow in southern China, which many of Hong Kong's ancestry would have originated from. If you can get past the thought of oysters for breakfast, this dish is the PERFECT HANGOVER CURE.

SERVES 8
Makes 2 medium 'cakes', perfect for feeding a hungry brunch crowd

100g (3½oz) small fresh pearl oysters (no shell)
3–4 teaspoons potato starch or cornflour (cornstarch)
vegetable oil, for deep-frying

THE BATTER
5 tablespoons plain (all-purpose) flour
1½ tablespoons sweet potato flour or yam flour
2 fresh eggs or 1 large duck egg
¼ teaspoon salt
¼ teaspoon white pepper
70ml (2½fl oz)/⅓ cup) water
1 spring onion (scallion)
3 sprigs of fresh coriander (cilantro)

TO SERVE
Chiu Chow chilli oil
fish sauce
limes

Wash the oysters in a mixing bowl under running water 2 or 3 times, then pour into a sieve and rub the potato starch or cornflour (cornstarch) gently around them to help rid them of any excess sand or grit. Wash them once more under running water to ensure they are cleaned thoroughly. Then half fill a wok with water and bring to the boil. Blanch the cleaned oysters in the boiling water for 1 minute and pour through a sieve.

Put the flours into a mixing bowl, then crack in the eggs and whisk well. Season with salt and pepper. Depending on the thickness of your batter, you'll want to add some or all of the 70ml (2½fl oz/⅓ cup) of water, ensuring that the batter is loose, but not watery. Finely chop the spring onion (scallion) and coriander (cilantro), add to the mixing bowl and whisk into the batter.

Place the blanched oysters in the batter and fold in gently.

Half-fill a wok or deep-fryer with vegetable oil and heat to 180°C (350°F), or use a wooden skewer or wooden chopstick to test by placing the tip in the oil: if the wood starts to fizz after a second or so, the oil is hot enough. Once the oil is at the right temperature, get ready to pour half the batter directly into the middle of the wok.

The idea of this dish is to make 2 big oyster cakes, so you must be prepared to pour half the mix into

the oil in one go, rather than bit by bit. Once you start pouring, do not stop until half the mix is in the wok and the fried oyster cake is intact. Do not stir the mix or oil at any point. Once the cake is formed, turn the heat down to medium and allow it to cook through for 2–3 minutes, basting the top of the cake with oil to cook it through well.

Once the bottom and sides of the cake have started to crisp up and turn golden brown, carefully flip it over and fry for a further 2–3 minutes. Once both sides are golden brown, the cake is cooked, and it will start to float at the top of the oil. Gently remove from the oil – the best way to go about this while keeping it intact is to use a slotted spoon or tongs (or both!) and place the cake carefully on a couple of sheets of kitchen paper to drain off any excess oil.

Repeat with the rest of the mix to make a second oyster cake.

Serve with Chiu Chow chilli oil or some fish sauce and lime juice on the side for dipping.

脆香魚皮

CRISPY FISH CRACKLING

SERVES 4 AS A SNACK

200g (7oz) cod skin (swapsies: any type of fish skin)
vegetable oil, for deep-frying

THE SEASONING CRUMB
1 teaspoon crushed Sichuan peppercorns
1 teaspoon salt
1 teaspoon sugar
2 teaspoons smoked paprika

Preheat the oven to 100°C/80°C fan (175°F). Lay the fish skin on kitchen paper, dabbing it with more kitchen paper to ensure all sides are completely dry. Place the skin, outer side down, on a piece of greaseproof paper on a roasting tray, and put it into the oven for 20 minutes to dry it out completely.

Meanwhile, mix the seasoning crumb ingredients together and set aside. After 20 minutes, remove the fish skin from the oven and slice it into bite-size pieces, ready to deep-fry.

Half-fill a large pot, wok or deep-fryer with vegetable oil and heat to 180°C (350°F), or use a wooden skewer or wooden chopstick to test by placing the tip in the oil: if the wood starts to fizz after a second or so, the oil is hot enough. Using a slotted spoon or a Chinese frying skimmer, carefully lay the pieces of dried fish skin in the oil. Once all the pieces are in, give them a gentle push to separate them completely. There will be an initial light crackling noise, and then the sizzling will start to slow down as the moisture is released from the pieces of skin. Deep-fry until the pieces are crisp and dry, about 3 minutes.

Once fried, place on a couple of pieces of kitchen paper to drain off any excess oil. Scatter the seasoning crumb over the crackling while the pieces are still hot, and give them a good shake around to distribute the seasoning evenly.

Serve as an alternative to crisps for a fun snack.

ROADSIDE BARBECUE PITS

Hong Kong's train and metro system is so efficient that it can almost make people forget that there are places to be visited and enjoyed outside the reach of the MTR and overground. Some of the best streetside eating in the city will in fact require you ditching the underground in favour of a minibus or taxi and possibly even some dreaded walking, but in my opinion it's an adventure worth taking!

Beachside barbecue pits around the Western Country Park can be rented, and along many of the more popular beaches around Sai Kung region you can get all the equipment and pre-marinated food you need to keep the barbecue going. These entrepreneurial restaurant owners have taken note of the true basics of Chinese cooking, where 90 per cent of the work is in the preparation (which they do for you), and the other 10 per cent is there for you to have fun, experiencing the food in a memorable environment: beachside or parkside, circling around a large barbecue pit. And what a great restaurant business it is too. Aside from the immense amount of marinating, there are almost no chefs required to run the restaurants! Genius.

With the food on offer at these barbecue joints, it's a given that most Hong Kong barbecues will involve quite a few processed foods, such as shop-bought fish cakes, frankfurters (Hong Kongers LOVE frankfurters), fishballs and meatballs of all kinds to suit the Hong Konger's love of processed meats and fish. If that's not your kind of food, however, you can dive straight into the meat section, where you will find fresh marinated steak, ribs, chops, chicken legs and wings, or a whole array of seafood; whatever takes your fancy.

The posher places are also a little more inventive and have straw mushrooms wrapped in thin slices of minute steak, whole garlic tiger prawns on a stick, poached octopus tentacles on a stick, curried tripe on a stick, fresh shiitake on a stick ... genuinely anything that can, pretty much will be thrown on to a stick when it comes to Hong Kong street food. In Sai Kung, you can actually head over to the pier, where there are fishermen selling freshly caught fish and seafood, pick up what you want and then take it to the barbecue joints to cook up on the fire.

And as the stick-loving street food culture brings us back to the busier streets of Hong Kong, it's not just the beachsides that embrace the barbecue culture and love of raw fire. There are still some local streetside hot pot places around Kowloon City and Temple Street that have their hot pots cooking on outdoor coal-fired table-top buckets, where the claypots are interchangeable with small table-top grills, allowing you to barbecue whatever you want at your table. During the winter months, when locals are less inclined to sit outside to eat, streetside sweet potato stands pop out of nowhere to warm you up, with their coal pits roasting chestnuts on the top, and a secret built-in 'oven' that's busily slow-cooking a box full of sweet potatoes below. Hong Kong people love to eat simple food like this, where the natural flavour and texture is perfect as it is.

頂級燒烤醬

ULTIMATE BARBECUE SAUCE

MY OWN TRICK when barbecuing is to make one large batch of base sauce that can be used as a glaze, a sauce, a marinade or a dressing. You might only need other ingredient to change the taste of each skewer, depending on what you are cooking on the grill. THERE IS BEAUTY IN SIMPLICITY. Every different ingredient that you put on a skewer or bamboo stick will have its own unique flavour, and this particular base sauce will help to ACCENTUATE THE FLAVOUR without overpowering its natural taste.

MAKES 1 JAR

4 cloves of garlic
a thumb-size piece of ginger, peeled
2 bird's-eye chillies
2 spring onions (scallions)
10 sprigs of fresh coriander (cilantro)
2 teaspoons English mustard
10 tablespoons light soy sauce
4 tablespoons dark soy sauce
2 tablespoons rice vinegar
3 tablespoons sugar
2 teaspoons pure sesame oil

Finely chop the garlic, ginger, chillies, spring onions (scallions) and coriander (cilantro) and place in a mixing bowl or jug. Add the mustard, light and dark soy, rice vinegar, sugar and sesame oil and stir well. Cover and let the flavours combine for at least 1 hour, or overnight for best results.

金菇牛肉卷

ENOKI BEEF WRAP

MAKES 5

10 asparagus stalks
300g (10½oz) enoki mushrooms
10 minute steaks, or very thinly sliced
rib-eye steak

THE MARINADE

1 tablespoon black pepper sauce
(available in Chinese supermarkets)
5 tablespoons Ultimate Barbecue
Sauce (see page 36)

TO COOK

5 bamboo skewers

Soak the bamboo skewers completely in cold water for at least 30 minutes.

Wrap 1 asparagus stalk and a small clump of enoki mushrooms with 1 piece of minute steak or thinly cut rib-eye steak, and roll it up, like making cannoli, except swapping the pasta for a piece of beef (you can also buy thin slices of beef for hot pot from Chinese supermarkets). Repeat the wrapping with the rest of the asparagus, mushrooms and beef, then skewer 2 beef wraps on to each skewer.

Place in a roasting tray. Mix the marinade ingredients together in a bowl and rub all over the wraps.

Place the beef skewers on a hot barbecue (roughly 200–220°C/ 400–425°F) for 2 minutes on each side, then serve alongside the rest of the barbecue stick suggestions that follow.

煨番薯

ROASTED SWEET POTATO

**SERVES 2, OR 4 WITH ADDITIONAL
SIDES OR BARBECUED MEATS**

1 tablespoon vegetable oil
1 teaspoon sea salt
2 whole sweet potatoes
6 tablespoons Ultimate Barbecue
Sauce (see page 36)

Rub the vegetable oil and salt around the outside of the sweet potatoes. Then wrap both sweet potatoes completely in foil.

Place the sweet potatoes directly on the coals of a medium-hot fire (roughly 160–170°C/325–340°F) and cook for 45 minutes to 1 hour, turning every 10 minutes.

Serve with the Ultimate Barbecue Sauce on the side, to drizzle over the sweet potato flesh while eating.

香菇串

SHIITAKE ON A STICK

MAKES 20

300g (10½oz) fresh shiitake
mushrooms

THE GLAZE
6 tablespoons Ultimate Barbecue
Sauce (see page 36)
1 tablespoon crushed soy bean
paste (swapsies: miso paste)
3 tablespoons vegetable stock

TO COOK
20 bamboo skewers

Soak the bamboo skewers
completely in cold water for at
least 30 minutes.

Skewer 3 or 4 shiitake mushrooms
on to each stick. Mix the glaze
ingredients together in a bowl,
ready to brush on to the mushrooms
when grilling. The vegetable stock
will thin out the sauce and allow
the mushrooms to develop a
slow caramelized flavour, rather
than causing them to burn on
the outside.

Place the mushroom skewers
on a medium-hot fire (roughly
160–170°C/325–340°F) for
5 minutes, basting continuously
with the glaze and turning when
it catches fire. Serve alongside
the rest of the barbecue stick
suggestions on pages 37–42.

Pictured overleaf

咖哩章魚鬚

CURRIED OCTOPUS TENTACLE

SERVES 4

4–5 octopus tentacles

THE POACHING LIQUID
1 star anise
1 cinnamon stick
2 cloves
2 bay leaves
1 litre (1¾ pints/4 cups) fresh
　chicken stock
1 litre (1¾ pints/4 cups) hot water
¼ teaspoon turmeric
½–1 teaspoon sea salt

THE MARINADE
3 teaspoons curry powder
½ teaspoon chilli powder
12 tablespoons Ultimate Barbecue
　Sauce (see page 36)

TO COOK
4–5 bamboo skewers

Place the star anise, cinnamon stick, cloves and bay leaves in a large saucepan and bring to a medium heat, then dry-fry for 1 minute, turning the spices once or twice so as not to burn them.

Once you start to smell the aroma of the heated spices, add the chicken stock, hot water, turmeric and sea salt and bring to the boil. Put the octopus tentacles into the poaching liquid and turn the heat down to a simmer. Simmer for 45 minutes to 1 hour, to soften the octopus meat.

Mix the marinade ingredients together in a bowl. Skewer each tentacle with a bamboo skewer, then massage the marinade well into the tentacles.

Place the octopus skewers on a hot fire (roughly 200–220°C/400–425°F) for 3 minutes on each side. Once well charred on the outside, baste with any leftover marinade and serve alongside the rest of the barbecue stick suggestions on pages 37–42.

Pictured overleaf

蒜蓉辣椒老虎蝦

GARLIC & CHILLI TIGER PRAWNS

SERVES 5

10 large raw tiger prawns

THE MARINADE
2 cloves of garlic
1 teaspoon Chiu Chow chilli oil (or
  homemade chilli oil, see page 146)
3 tablespoons melted salted butter
10 tablespoons Ultimate Barbecue
  Sauce (see page 36)

TO COOK
10 bamboo skewers

Soak the bamboo skewers completely in cold water for at least 30 minutes.

Finely slice the garlic, then mix together with the rest of the marinade ingredients in a roasting tray big enough to fit the prawns on sticks.

Butterfly the prawns using scissors, starting from the top, between the head and the body, and cutting down the spine of the prawn all the way to the tail. Once the shell is opened up, run a sharp knife through to butterfly the prawn further. Then press the 2 sides of the prawn down to butterfly completely. Now slice horizontally 6–8 times along the meat of the prawn body, as if scoring the prawn. This will open up the prawn so that all the flavour from the marinade goes in nicely and it's easy to peel once cooked.

Poke a skewer through each prawn, all the way upwards and through the base of the head to keep it tight on the skewer. Place all the skewered prawns in a roasting tray and baste with as much of the marinade as possible.

Place the prawn skewers on a hot fire (roughly 200–220°C/400–425°F) for 3 minutes on each side. Once well charred on the outside, baste with any leftover marinade and serve alongside the rest of the barbecue stick suggestions on pages 37–41.

CHA CHAAN TENGS

If I were to paint a picture of Hong Kong, I would always start with the best places to eat. Eat your way through Hong Kong in the right way, and you get a true sense of the city and the people who live there. Put out of your mind the high-end sprawling shopping centres, Monopoly-like high-rises of hotels and trendy restaurants. The heart of Hong Kong does not float high in the air, but rather is nestled down at street level, crowd level. The real fun starts with the *cha chaan tengs!*

The best way to describe a *cha chaan teng* is to combine one part UK greasy spoon, with its simplicity of uncomplicated sandwiches, fry-ups and builder's tea, with one part US diner: think Formica booth seating, bright fluorescent lighting and comforting home-cooked style dishes. Bear in mind that this does not describe the food itself, but rather the essence of the environment and its function.

Cha chaan tengs, directly translated as 'tea house lounges', were created after the Second World War and were based on the desire to make accessible what were often prohibitively expensive, and sometimes downright racist, establishments that served Western-style food

only to Westerners, or to those with the funds to buy their way in. Post-war, the quintessentially British tea and cake culture and consumption saw such a surge in Hong Kong that there needed to be a new affordable eatery that could accommodate this practice, knocking Western food off the pedestal it had been placed on due to its exclusivity. Given the hustle and bustle of the city, there was also the great need to focus on simplicity and quick service in order to serve busy locals. Thus the *cha chaan teng* was born.

Some of the signature dishes of the *cha chaan teng* include condensed milk on heavily buttered toast, macaroni soups topped with spam and a fried egg, crusty roll sandwiches (much like the Pork Chop Crusty Roll on page 16) that straddle a Western school tuck-shop crisp sandwich roll, and a fluffy steamed Eastern *bao*. All to be washed down by the milkiest 'cuppa tea' – made with condensed milk, of course.

It may sound like the clunkiest of combinations, I realize, but trust me when I say that these eateries serve delicious and honestly comforting food and will be one of the best cultural experiences you can have when visiting Hong Kong.

餃子及包點
DUMPLINGS & BAOS

水餃皮

SHUI GAO DOUGH (SIMPLE ROLLING & CHINESE ROLLING TECHNIQUE)

If you have never made them before, dumplings can be one of the most daunting things to tackle in the kitchen. Once you get going, however, and learn a FEW SIMPLE FOLDS, you'll find it easier to pick up more intricate techniques. The key is to start small and simple, and little by little work your way up. If you are making dumplings for the first time, I suggest using ready-made dough. You can find it both fresh and frozen in most Chinese supermarkets. It really is the best way to start to BUILD YOUR DUMPLING-MAKING CONFIDENCE. For the more experienced dumpling maker (or for those who are that unique combination of brave and ballsy), try this simple recipe for a great all-round dumpling dough. It's completely interchangeable in any of the following dumpling recipes and will make a DELICIOUS MEAL, whatever the filling.

MAKES 25–30 DUMPLINGS

THE DOUGH
250g (9oz/about 1¾ cups) medium-gluten wheat flour, or plain flour (all-purpose flour)
25g (1oz) tapioca flour
a pinch of salt
170ml (6fl oz/¾ cup) boiling water
25g (1oz) vegetable oil

Put the flour, tapioca flour and salt into a large mixing bowl. Using a spatula or a wooden spoon, gradually mix in the boiling water, until all the flour has come away from the sides of the bowl. Lastly, add the oil, then start to knead the dough well by hand for 5 minutes. Alternatively, you can use an electric dough mixer fitted with a dough hook attachment; start on a low speed for the first minute or so, then knead well on a high speed for 2–3 minutes.

Once you have a smooth dough, form it into a ball, scraping the dough off the sides of the mixing bowl. Rub with a little oil, put it back into the bowl, then cover with a damp tea towel and allow to rest for 10 minutes.

If making the dough itself is as adventurous as you want to be for now (or if you're just too hungry to have patience), rolling out the dough into 2 or 3 large pieces, as thin as possible, and taking a 7cm (2¾ inch) square or round biscuit cutter (depending on the recipe and the shape you would like to fold) to it is the best way forward.

However, if you are now thinking you are closer to becoming a dumpling maverick, the traditional way to roll a round dumpling pastry is to roll each and every piece of dough into an individual sheet. This is usually done with a specific *dim sum* rolling pin, a thin wooden stick that looks very much like the end of a broom, and sometimes even thinner.

If you are inclined to become a true *dim sum* master, here's how to practise the right movement:

First, roll a third of the rested dough into a long cylinder, roughly 1.5cm (⅝ inch) thick, keeping the remainder of the dough covered so it doesn't dry out. Cut the cylinder into 1cm (½ inch) chunks.

Roll each piece of dough into a small ball and set aside. Before rolling each individual piece, dust the work surface with a good amount of plain flour (all-purpose flour) or medium-gluten wheat flour. Take a piece of dough and push down on it with your palm to form a small circle. With the dough still resting on the floured surface, with your left or non-dominant hand, using your thumb and fingers underneath the edge of the dough, begin to turn the dough anti-clockwise, with the base of the pastry sitting on the surface at all

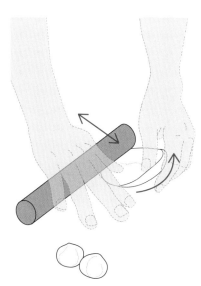

times. (I use my middle finger as the 'hub' to the wheel of pastry.)

While you are turning the pastry, using your right or dominant hand along with a small rolling pin, with a relevant amount of force roll inwards towards the centre of the forming circle, allowing your pressure to ease up when rolling outwards towards the edges of the circle. Turn the pastry anti-clockwise with your non-dominant hand and continue this rolling process, eventually forming a small circle with a slightly thicker hump of dough in the middle. This thickness will help to protect the filling from breaking through the thin pastry, keeping your dumpling perfectly intact.

COOKING METHOD

The same cooking method can be used for all of the dumpling shapes that follow.

Fill a large pot or wok with water, add a pinch of salt and bring to the boil. Gently add your dumplings and boil for 3–4 minutes, or until they begin to float to the surface, signalling they are cooked. Remove using a spider or slotted spoon and serve with the following dipping sauce.

DIPPING SAUCE
½ teaspoon Chiu Chow chilli oil
1 tablespoon oyster sauce
½ tablespoon light soy sauce
100ml (3½fl oz/⅓ cup) chicken stock (or Classic Chinese broth, see page 57)

Combine the dipping sauce ingredients in a small pan, mixing well. Gently heat, reducing the sauce slightly, then pour into a dipping bowl and serve with fresh dumplings.

白菜甘藍餃

PAK CHOI & KALE DUMPLING: THE FAT CAT FOLD

MAKES 25–30

25–30 ready-made round dumpling pastries, or thinly rolled circles of *shui gao* dough (see page 50)

THE FILLING
2 medium or 1 large *pak choi*
5–6 large kale leaves
1 clove of garlic
½ a thumb-size piece of ginger
1 spring onion (scallion)
5 sprigs of fresh coriander (cilantro)
100g (3½oz) minced pork (swapsies: extra firm, fresh tofu for vegetarians)

THE MARINADE
½ teaspoon salt
½ teaspoon sugar
½ tablespoon pure sesame oil

Finely chop the *pak choi*, kale, garlic, ginger, spring onion (scallion) and coriander (cilantro) and place in a large mixing bowl, then add the minced pork and the marinade ingredients and mix well.

To make the fat cat fold, place one dumpling pastry flat on a clean surface. Place roughly 1 teaspoon of the marinated mix in the centre of the pastry.

Dab a little water all around the edge of the pastry, then fold the top of the pastry over the filling until it meets the bottom edge and press down, closing the edges of the pastry to make a half-moon shape.

Now, holding the side edges of the pastry, with the half-moon still pointing downwards, pull the 2 edges (cat ears) upwards to meet in the middle, creating a 'fat cat' shape.

Lastly, overlap the 2 top corners of the fat cat shaped pastry together and stick together with another dab of water, pinching together tightly.

Do the same with the rest of the pastries and filling. To cook, see page 51.

芹菜蘑菇餃

CELERY & MUSHROOM DUMPLING: THE SMILING NUN FOLD

MAKES 25–30

25–30 ready-made Shanghai dumpling pastries (square) or thinly rolled squares of *shui gao* dough (see page 50)

THE FILLING
50g (1¾oz) dried shiitake mushrooms
200g (7oz) Chinese celery (swapsies: Western celery)
50g (1¾oz) Tian Jin preserved Chinese cabbage (optional)
1 clove of garlic
½ a thumb-size piece of ginger
1 spring onion (scallion)
5 sprigs of fresh coriander (cilantro)
100g minced pork

THE MARINADE
1 teaspoon salt
1 teaspoon sugar
½ tablespoon pure sesame oil

Soak the shiitake mushrooms in hot water overnight, or for at least 2 hours, then drain.

Finely chop the mushrooms, celery, cabbage, garlic, ginger, spring onion (scallion) and coriander (cilantro) and place in a large mixing bowl. Add the minced pork and the marinade ingredients and mix well.

To make the smiling nun fold, place one of the pastries on a flat surface in front of you. Place roughly 1½ teaspoons of the marinated mix in the centre of the pastry.

Fold the bottom edge of the pastry over the filling, flush to the top edge, then press down on the top edge to lightly seal. Tightly roll the filling over towards the top edge once, forming a sausage roll or cigar shape, but keeping the corners of the wrapper still free.

Press down on the edges of the pastry either side of the filling, to stick them together.

Now pick up the edges of the pastry, holding the innermost pleats or corners. Overlap the inside pleats over one another, using a little water to help them stick, pinching and squeezing the edges tight.

Leaving the outer unfolded edges open should make the dumpling look like a slightly podgy-looking 'nun', with a gummy smile, when turned on its side.

Do the same with the rest of the pastries and filling. To cook, see page 51.

西洋菜餃

WATERCRESS DUMPLING:
THE UNHAPPY FISH FOLD

MAKES 25–30

25–30 ready-made round dumpling pastries, or thinly rolled circles of *shui gao* dough (see page 50)

THE FILLING
200g (7oz) watercress
1 clove of garlic
½ a thumb-size piece of ginger
1 spring onion (scallion)
5 sprigs of fresh coriander (cilantro)
100g (3½oz/¾ cup) raw, peeled and deveined prawns (shrimp)
50g (1¾oz) minced pork

THE MARINADE
½ tablespoon oyster sauce
½ teaspoon salt
1 teaspoon sugar
1 teaspoon light soy sauce
½ tablespoon pure sesame oil

Finely chop the watercress, garlic, ginger, spring onion (scallion), coriander (cilantro) and prawns (shrimp) and place in a large mixing bowl. Add the minced pork along with the marinade ingredients, and mix well.

To make the unhappy fish fold, take one pastry and place it flat on your work surface in front of you. Place roughly 1½ teaspoons of the marinated mix in the centre of the pastry. Before picking the dumpling up, wet the edges of the pastry with water to help them stick together.

Fold the dumpling in half, pinching the pastry together in just the far right-hand corner, cupping the base of the filling with your middle to pinky fingers and freeing your thumb and index finger up to help pleat. Using your dominant hand and holding your thumb on the outside bottom of the pastry, create pencil pleat after pencil pleat of pastry, one on top of the other, in much the same way a curtain folds when drawn along a rail, using your non-dominant thumb and index finger to help press the pleats together.

Keep folding the pleats over each other, until you have pleated the entire length of the pastry, keeping your filling in the centre. When you are ready to close the dumpling, pinch the left-hand edge closed and lightly pull downwards at the 2 ends of your newly created seal of pleats to form an 'unhappy goldfish' shape.

Do the same with the rest of the pastries and filling. To cook, see page 51.

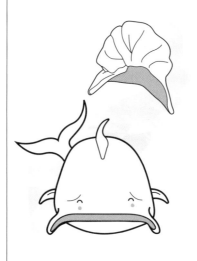

上湯餃

SHEUNG TONG GAO (PLACE ON TOP OF SOUP LARGE DUMPLING)

SERVES 8 PEOPLE AS A STARTER

THE CLASSIC CHINESE BROTH
500g (1lb 2oz) chicken wings
300g (10½oz) pork ribs

THE CLARIFYING MIX
100g (3½oz) wind-dried
  Chinese ham
1 thumb-size piece of ginger
4 spring onions (scallions)
1 piece of dried mandarin peel
10 black peppercorns
1 clove
1 star anise
2 tablespoons light soy sauce
300g (10½oz) minced pork, mixed
  with 2 egg whites
1 teaspoon salt, to season at the end

THE DUMPLINGS
8 balls of *shui gao* dough (roughly
  25g/1oz each) (see page 50)
½ a recipe's worth of any of the
  fillings from the previous
  3 dumpling recipes
1 spring onion (scallion), chopped,
  to garnish

To make the broth, first place the chicken wings and pork ribs in a large stockpot or saucepan and pour boiling water over them to cover. Bring to the boil, then reduce the heat and simmer for 5 minutes. Take off the heat and pour away the water and any scum that has come to the surface. Under the tap, rinse the meat with cold water to get rid of any residual scum or impurities.

Now add the clarifying mix ingredients to the stockpot and pour in cold water to come three-quarters of the way up the pan. Bring the stock to the boil, then turn the heat down to low and simmer gently, uncovered, for 2 hours. You are essentially making a clear stock, similar to a French consommé with these ingredients, so do not feel obligated to break up the mince. In fact, if left in one piece the overcooked minced meat will make a beautifully flavoured addition to the Fragrant Aubergine (Eggplant) with Minced Pork on page 80. Once the stock has simmered for 2 hours, remove from the heat and pass once or twice through a sieve until you have a clean broth. Return to the pot and bring up to a medium heat.

To make the dumplings, roll out 8 large circular dumpling pastries, roughly 8cm (3¼ inches) in diameter (see page 50 for the rolling technique, or use a biscuit cutter).

Fill each circular pastry with 1½ tablespoons of your chosen filling mix.

Fold the dumplings in any shape you wish. For ease, you can simply gather the pastry together at the top and crimp so it looks like a drawstring money bag, taking care to pinch the top tightly to ensure that the pastry is well sealed and not too thick so it sticks together well.

You can either cook the dumplings directly in the stock, or fill a separate saucepan three-quarters of the way up with salted water and bring to the boil. Either way, add your dumplings carefully, one at a time, and boil for 5 minutes, or until they start to float. Once the dumplings are floating, allow them to simmer for a further minute, then scoop out using a slotted spoon, add to your delicious broth, and serve, garnished with chopped spring onion.

雲吞燴蟹子麵

WONTON BRAISED NOODLES WITH TOBIKO: THE JELLY FISH FOLD

MAKES 25 WONTONS / SERVES 4

25 fresh wonton pastries
400ml (14fl oz/1¾ cups) classic
   Chinese broth (see page 57)
300g (10½oz) fresh, fine egg noodles
   (swapsies: dried fine egg noodles,
   soaked in hot water for 3 minutes
   and drained)
1 tablespoon oyster sauce
½ tablespoon light soy sauce
20g orange tobiko, optional (flying
   fish roe, from sushi specialists)
spring onions (scallions), finely sliced,
   to garnish

THE FILLING
4 dried shiitake mushrooms
1 spring onion (scallion)
½ a thumb-size piece of ginger
200g (7oz/1½ cups) raw, peeled
   and deveined prawns (shrimp)
100g (3½oz) minced pork

THE MARINADE
1 tablespoon oyster sauce
¼ teaspoon salt
1 teaspoon sugar
½ teaspoon pure sesame oil
½ tablespoon cornflour (cornstarch)

Soak the shiitake mushrooms in hot water overnight or for a minimum of 2 hours, then drain. Finely chop them along with the spring onion (scallion) and ginger and place in a mixing bowl.

Lightly bash the prawns (shrimp) with the side of your cleaver or knife, keeping them whole, but making them more flexible, which will make it easier to wrap the wontons. Lastly, add the pork mince, along with the prawns and the marinade ingredients to the bowl and mix everything together well.

Traditionally, the mix is pounded into a uniform paste by cupping one hand, picking up the mix, and throwing it back into the bowl. This helps to tenderize the meat and knocks out air pockets in the paste. You can also use an electric mixer for the same effect; using the k-hook attachment, place the marinated mix in the mixer and beat on a low-medium speed for 2 minutes.

To make the jelly fish shaped dumplings you will need to use what I call the croc fold. Place a wonton pastry on a flat surface, positioning it in a diamond shape straight ahead of you. Place 1 teaspoon of mix in the centre of the pastry.

Fold one corner vertically, over the opposite corner, to form a slightly lopsided triangle. Hold the dumpling up by the top of the triangle with your non-dominant hand. Shape your dominant hand into a 'crocodile

jaw' shape, where your thumb is the lower jaw and your index finger is the upper jaw.

Start to feed the pastry into the jaws of the croc, squeezing the pastry together into the webbing of your thumb, creating rough pleats as you gather the excess pastry together in your croc's jaws. Continue feeding until the dumpling is fully closed. Then pinch the pastry tightly along the top of the filling. Do not be scared to clamp down hard, so that the filling is well and truly sealed inside the pastry.

Now bring the broth of your choice (or alternatively 400ml/14fl oz/1¾ cups of water with 1 teaspoon of salt added) to the boil. Drop in your noodles and blanch for 1½ minutes, then fish them out carefully with tongs and place in a bowl.

Next, boil the wontons (usually 5–6 per serving) in the same water or broth for 4 minutes, until they begin to float. Remove the wontons to a separate bowl, using a slotted spoon or a Chinese skimmer, then bring the water or soup back to the boil.

Just before serving, dunk the noodles (either fresh, or dried and soaked) back into the soup or boiling water for 30 seconds, then put them back into their bowl and add the oyster sauce and light soy sauce. Mix well, then divide the noodles between

individual serving bowls (they will be the base of the dish). Place the hot wontons on top of the noodles and scatter 2 teaspoons of flying fish roe over the top of each portion. Garnish with finely sliced rings of spring onion (scallion).

Serve with a bowl of broth (my favourite homemade stock is on page 57 or try the simple stock from page 85) on the side and some lightly blanched green vegetables, such as lettuce leaves or any type of Chinese greens.

香脆鮮蝦蘆筍豆腐卷

CRISPY TOFU ROLL WITH PRAWNS (SHRIMP) & ASPARAGUS

12 whole raw, peeled and deveined prawns (shrimp)
6 asparagus stalks
1 egg, beaten, for brushing
2 large sheets of tofu skin (you can find these at many Asian supermarkets)
vegetable oil, for frying

THE MINCED FILLING
2 dried shiitake mushrooms
6 green beans
1 clove of garlic
1 spring onion (scallion)
200g (7oz/1½ cups) raw, peeled and deveined prawns (shrimp)
100g (3½oz) white fish fillet

THE MARINADE
1 tablespoon oyster sauce
½ teaspoon sugar
¼ teaspoon salt
1 teaspoon pure sesame oil

THE DIPPING SAUCE
2 tablespoons light soy sauce
6 tablespoons Chingkiang black vinegar

Soak the shiitake mushrooms in hot water overnight or for at least 2 hours, then drain.

Top and tail the green beans, then finely chop with the garlic, spring onion (scallion) and mushrooms. Finely chop the 200g (7oz/1½ cups) prawns (shrimp) for the minced filling, and the white fish, or, mince in a food processor. Place all these in a large mixing bowl and mix in the marinade ingredients until evenly combined.

Butterfly the 12 whole prawns, then score horizontally 5 or 6 times across each prawn to flatten them. Halve the asparagus stalks lengthways, then cut them into 2–3cm (¾–1¾ inch) pieces. Have the beaten egg and a brush ready.

Now you are ready for rolling! Place a sheet of tofu skin on a large chopping board, squarely aligned to you, and start to line up the separate tofu rolls as follows. You'll want the skin to be about 20–24cm (8–9¾ inches) long, so feel free to cut it if there is more than this.

Starting on the far left-hand side, place 1 tablespoon of filling 1cm (½ inch) from both the bottom and side edge of the tofu skin. Continuing in a horizontal line and leaving roughly 1–2cm (½–¾ inches) between the mounds of filling, line up another 4–5 tablespoons of filling, moving across the tofu skin until you reach the far edge.

Place a butterflied prawn horizontally on top of each mound of filling, and place 2 pieces of asparagus horizontally on either side of the butterflied prawn.

Brush the naked tofu skin generously with the beaten egg, including in between the mounds of filling. This will help to ensure the tofu rolls stick together well.

Now, from the bottom up, fold the tofu skin and the mounds of mixture tightly once over, similar to rolling up a spring roll, covering the filling completely. Press the top of the tofu skin firmly in between the mounds of filling to stick the skin together, creating individual rolls in the process. Roll the entire long row of tofu skin over itself, brush with eggwash, then repeat, until you have come to the end of the sheet.

Lastly, with the tip of a sharp knife or cleaver, cut in between each mound of filling where the tofu skin should be stuck together in layers, creating individual rolls. Repeat with the rest of the tofu skin and filling. It's OK if the sides of the rolls are slightly open – the rustic finish of this dish is part of its appeal.

Heat 2 tablespoons of vegetable oil to a medium heat in a large frying pan. Once hot, place the individual tofu rolls in the frying pan and fry for 3–4 minutes on each side, until golden brown. Mix together the dipping sauce ingredients and serve with the rolls.

包類
BAO
DOUGH

包類款式
MAKING
BAO SHAPES

Fluffy, pillowy white *baos* hit China, Hong Kong and Japan many years ago, but it wasn't until recently that they became a MAINSTREAM STREET SNACK in the West. With our clear love of burgers and all things bread, it's no wonder these softer, slightly sweeter breads are so MOREISH, no matter where in the world we are. The airy texture is great for mopping up sauces, while their firmness makes them the perfect bun to keep a sandwich together. This simple *bao* dough recipe will get you going, but be warned, trying out new shapes is addictive!

MAKES 10 LARGE OR 16–20 MINI BAO

THE DRY MIX
530g (1lb 3oz/4 cups) middle-gluten wheat flour (swapsies: plain flour/all-purpose flour), plus extra for dusting
½ teaspoon salt
7g (just under ¼oz or 1 sachet) fast-action dried yeast
40g (1½oz) caster sugar (superfine sugar)
15g (½oz) baking powder

THE LIQUID
50ml (2fl oz) milk
200–250ml (7–8fl oz/about 1 cup) warm water (depending on how humid your room feels – if the air feels very dry you'll want to add a little more water, but if it is very humid, less is required)
25ml (1fl oz) vegetable or sunflower oil

Put the dry mix ingredients into the bowl of a free-standing mixer fitted with a dough hook attachment.

Mix the liquid ingredients in a measuring jug. Then slowly pour the liquid into the mixer while kneading on a low speed for around 2 minutes, until all the water is mixed into the flour. Once combined, turn the speed up to high for a further 2 minutes, until the dough has a smooth yet tacky feel to it.

Once the dough has been well kneaded, dust it with 2 tablespoons of flour. Shape the dough into a rough ball, scraping off any additional dough on the sides of the bowl, then coat it lightly with 1 tablespoon of vegetable oil, put it back into the bowl, cover with a damp cloth and leave aside in a warm, preferably moist, draught-free location (such as inside a room-temperature oven) for 1–1½ hours.

Once the dough has doubled in size, you can make it into whatever shapes you wish before steaming. Steaming time will vary between 8 and 15 minutes, depending on the shape and size of your finished buns (the thinner the bun, the shorter the steaming time).

This *bao* dough is classically a type of steamed bread dough that originated from northern China for making breads such as *mantou* (a pure steamed bread for mopping up sauces) or *baozi* (a filled steamed bread). It is a simple yeast dough that rises over time when proved at the right temperature, making it much easier to make than most people think. After the first 1½ hours of proving, the dough can be shaped into burgers, *hirata* buns, or even more classic dumpling shapes, to hold whatever filling suits you best. Here are some simple shapes to start with, followed by some delicious fillings you can use to mix and match your *baos*.

HIRATA BAO: THE SANDWICH
Roll the proved *bao* dough out until completely flat and roughly 4mm (¼ inch) in thickness, then cut into either rectangles or circles. If cutting circles, roll them out again once cut, to make elongated oval shapes. Once all the shapes have been cut, lightly brush the top of each one with a dab of vegetable oil. Place an oiled chopstick across the centre of each piece of dough and fold one side over the top to form a 'lip', then remove the chopstick. Once you have made the sandwich shapes, cover with a damp cloth and set aside to rest for 15–20 minutes.

BURGER BAO: THE SLIDER
To make a burger-shaped *bao*, roll the proved *bao* dough into a long cylinder, roughly 3–4cm

THE SLIDER

THE BAO MASTER

THE SANDWICH

THE SNOWBALL

(1¼–1½ inches) in diameter, then cut the cylinder into 3–4cm (1¼–1½ inch) thick pieces. Roll each piece of dough in your hands to form a smooth ball. Take a ball of dough and press down firmly with the palm of your hand to form a flattened circle. Brush with a little dab of vegetable oil, then place another piece of dough on top. Slightly dome or cup your hand and press down once more to form the 2 halves of your burger bun shape, the bottom bun being completely flat and the top being domed. Repeat until all the dough has been used. Once you have made your burger *bao* shapes, cover with a damp cloth and set aside to rest for 15–20 minutes.

FILLED BAO: THE SNOWBALL

Putting filling into a *bao* takes a little practice. First, much like the burger bao fold, roll the proved *bao* dough into a long cylinder, roughly 3–4cm

(1¼–1½ inches) in diameter, then cut the cylinder into 3–4cm (1¼–1½ inch) thick pieces. Roll each piece of dough in your hands to form a smooth ball. Take a ball of dough and press down firmly with the palm of your hand to form a flattened circle. Then run your thumbs and index fingers around the outside of the circle of dough, while pressing down relatively firmly, to make the circle big enough to place a teaspoon or so of filling inside. Once you have added the filling of your choice, hold the dough lightly in the cupped fingertips of your non-dominant hand. Now, using the thumb and index finger of your dominant hand, start to bring the sides of the dough up around the sides of the filling until you are able to close the filled bao entirely. Tightly pinch the dough together at the top of the bao, while twisting the very top and maintaining a smooth sphere around the sides. Turn it over

once and place on the work surface, twisted side down. Cover with a damp cloth and set aside to rest for a further 15–20 minutes.

TRADITIONAL BAO: THE BAO MASTER

This fold is for those who want to become true *bao* masters and are equally ready for moments of frustration before getting it right. It takes work, but in my opinion it's work worth doing.

Rolling the dough

First, roll a third of the rested dough into a long cylinder, roughly 2.5cm (1 inch) thick, keeping the remainder of the dough covered so it doesn't dry out. Cut the cylinder into 2.5cm (1 inch) chunks, then roll each piece of dough into a small ball and set aside.

Dust a work surface with a good amount of plain flour (all-purpose flour) or medium-gluten wheat flour.

Take a piece of dough and push down on to it to form a small circle. With the dough still resting on the floured surface, with your left hand or non-dominant hand, using your thumb and fingers underneath the edge of the dough, begin to turn the dough anticlockwise, with the base of the pastry sitting on the surface at all times. (I use my middle finger as the 'hub' to the wheel of pastry.)

While you are turning the pastry, using your right or dominant hand along with a small rolling pin, with a relevant amount of force roll inwards towards the centre of the forming circle, allowing the pressure to ease up when rolling outwards towards the edges of the circle. Turn the pastry clockwise with your non-dominant hand and continue this rolling process, eventually forming a small circle with a slightly thicker hump of dough in the middle of the pastry. This thickness will help to protect the filling from breaking through the thin pastry, keeping your dumpling perfectly intact.

Folding the dough – the money bag pleat

Place 1 teaspoon or so of filling in the centre of the dough, holding the dough lightly in the fingertips of your non-dominant hand. Holding your thumb on the outside and towards the base of the pastry, carefully create pencil pleat after pencil pleat of pastry, one on top of each other, much like how a curtain folds when drawn along a rail, taking care not to rip the pastry, turning the *bao* slowly with your non-dominant hand so the pleats wrap around the entire dumpling.

Keep folding over each other until you get halfway around the pastry with your pleats, keeping your left thumb lightly over the top of the filling to keep it in the centre of your pastry and stop it falling out.

Once you have reached halfway, tilt your non-dominant hand, the one that is holding the pastry, slightly upwards, as if giving yourself a 'thumbs up' while staring at the inside of your fingertips. Now continue with the pencil pleats, using your dominant thumb and index finger, by twisting into the pastry and continuing to pinch the outside together to form the pleats. Continue with the pleat until you get to the end of your pastry, then twist into the top of the pastry once or twice and pinch the centre of the dough together to seal the *bao* and make 'the money bag' shape.

If you get this far, give yourself a pat on the back and repeat until you have used all the dough. Cover the *bao* shapes with a damp cloth and set aside to rest for a further 15–20 minutes.

COOKING METHOD

The same cooking method is used for all of the *bao* shapes.

Place *bao* on squares of greaseproof paper and then steam for 8–15 minutes (depending on the size of your *bao*) in a covered steam basket, inside a wok half-filled with boiling water, without opening the lid, until cooked through and risen well.

黑椒牛仔骨包

BLACK PEPPER GLAZED SHORT RIB BAO

Baos, burgers and sliders have been SETTING FOOD TRENDS around the world for years now. We tried a version of this slider in a new organic restaurant called Sohofama in Hong Kong, which seems to be LEADING THE WAY in urban farming and healthier cooking styles, while still managing to maintain the best part of traditional Chinese cooking techniques to create delicious dishes like this. When cooking this short rib *bao*, feel free to try out the different folds – the *hirata* bun fold or burger *bao* fold will both work well with the SLOW-COOKED SHORT RIB. Make sure you leave yourself plenty of time to make your *bao* dough and preferred *bao* shapes, steaming them just before you finish off the tender meat to make your LUXURIOUS BUNS.

SERVES 4

4 beef short ribs, separated
½ a portion of *bao* dough, ready to make 8–10 steamed *hirata* buns or burger *baos* (see page 62)

THE POACHING LIQUID
1 star anise
1 small cinnamon stick
2 cloves
2 bay leaves
1 teaspoon black peppercorns
½ teaspoon salt
1 litre (1 ¾ pints/4 cups) water

THE GLAZE
3 tablespoons jarred Chinese black pepper sauce (available in Chinese supermarkets)
2 tablespoons light soy sauce
4 teaspoons sugar

Place the short ribs in a large saucepan and add all the poaching liquid ingredients. Bring to the boil on a high heat, then lower to a gentle simmer. Poach the beef ribs on a low heat for 3 hours, until the meat starts to fall off the bone but still keeps its shape.

While the meat is cooking, make your *bao* buns if you haven't made them beforehand.

Mix the glaze ingredients together in a large mixing bowl. Once the ribs have been poached, remove them from the poaching liquid and carefully remove the bones, leaving the meat itself whole and intact as much as possible.

Cut each long piece of meat in half vertically, in order to make more reasonably sized portions that will fit well into the steamed buns. Put the pieces of meat into the bowl of glaze and gently coat the pieces of meat, using a spoon to baste on all surfaces and sides.

Just before you finish glazing the meat, start steaming your *bao* buns (see page 65). Char each side of the meat under a hot grill (minimum 230°C/450°F) on a lined baking tray or unlined rack, or finish directly on the barbecue. Serve one piece of short rib to one steamed bun for ease of eating (with only moderate gluttony), along with some pickles or salad and condiments on the side.

香脆鮟鱇魚包

CRISPY MONKFISH CHEEK BAO

SERVES 4

½ a portion of *bao* dough, ready to
make 8–10 steamed *hirata* buns
or burger *baos* (see page 62)
20 fresh curry leaves
1 large fresh red chilli
1 clove of garlic
a pinch of salt
a pinch of cracked black pepper
8 large monkfish cheeks (off the bone
– ask your fishmonger to do this)
vegetable oil, for frying

THE BATTER

100g (3½oz/¾ cup) plain flour
(all-purpose flour)
20g (¾oz) cornflour (cornstarch)
1 teaspoon ground turmeric
½ teaspoon chilli powder
½ teaspoon salt
¼ teaspoon cracked black pepper
approx. 250ml (9fl oz/1 cup) very
cold soda water

Given the hands-on intensity of this
recipe, you will want to make and
steam your buns before beginning
the steps below. This way the *baos*
will be ready and waiting for the
crispy fish. To steam the buns, see
page 65.

Pick the curry leaves off their stems
and put them into a small bowl.
Roughly chop the red chilli into
thumbprint-size pieces and finely
chop the garlic, then add to the
bowl with a pinch of salt and
cracked black pepper.

Whisk the batter ingredients
together in a large mixing bowl until
smooth – it should be thin, with the
consistency of single cream.

Half-fill a large pot, wok or deep-
fryer with vegetable oil and heat to
180°C (350°F), or use a wooden
skewer or wooden chopstick to
test by placing the tip in the oil:
if the wood starts to fizz after a
second or two, the oil is hot enough.

Dip the monkfish cheeks into
the batter, then carefully put them
straight into the hot oil and fry for
5 or 6 minutes, or until golden
brown. The pieces should start to
float at the top of the oil after roughly
4–5 minutes. Allow a further minute
or two of frying once they start to
float, until they turn a golden brown.
Remove the fish pieces carefully
with a slotted spoon and drain
well on kitchen paper.

Lastly, heat ½ tablespoon of
vegetable oil in a wok to a high
heat. Once the oil is smoking hot,
add the garlic, chilli, curry leaves,
salt and pepper and immediately
add the fried monkfish cheeks. Toss
through once or twice, and serve
immediately by placing one piece
of fried fish inside each steamed *bao*.

TIP: TRY THESE BAOS WITH SOME
JAPANESE MAYONNAISE (AVAILABLE IN
ASIAN SUPERMARKETS) AND SRIRACHA
CHILLI SAUCE ON THE SIDE, ALONG WITH
SOME SALAD OF CHOICE TO TOP THE BAO.

小茴香牛肉蔥炸包

CUMIN BEEF & SPRING ONION (SCALLION) FRIED BAOS

SERVES 6–8

1 portion of *bao* dough, ready to make 20–25 *baos* (see page 62)
2 tablespoons vegetable oil

THE FILLING

50g (1¾oz) water chestnuts
1 clove of garlic
½ a thumb-size piece of ginger
5 sprigs of fresh coriander (cilantro)
3 spring onions (scallions)
200g (7oz) beef mince
1 egg yolk

THE MARINADE

1 tablespoon cumin seeds
½ teaspoon Chiu Chow chilli oil
1 tablespoon oyster sauce
½ teaspoon sugar
¼ teaspoon salt
1 teaspoon pure sesame oil

Finely chop the water chestnuts, garlic, ginger, coriander (cilantro) and 2 of the spring onions (scallions) and place in a large mixing bowl. Add the minced beef and egg yolk and mix well.

In a pan over a medium high heat, toast the cumin seeds until fragrant (30 seconds to 1 minute), then tip them into a mortar and gently crush, using a pestle. Add the crushed seeds to the filling mix, along with the other marinade ingredients, and stir to combine well.

After the *bao* dough has proved for 1½ hours, doubling in size, place the dough on a well-floured work surface and roll it out until approx. 5mm (¼ inch) in thickness. Finely chop the last spring onion and scatter the pieces over the dough. Using a cookie cutter (or the lip of a glass) approx. 7cm (2¾ inches) in diameter, cut the dough into as many pieces as possible.

Working with one piece of dough at a time, place 1½ teaspoons of filling into the centre of the pastry. Lift up the pastry and squeeze the edges together as if forming a drawstring money bag with your dominant hand. Holding the pastry in your dominant hand, twist the top tightly and continuously with the other hand, ensuring the filling does not leak out, until the pastry is completely sealed and you have a slightly swirled, spiralled effect at the top, and a well-rounded

dumpling below. Once well sealed, lightly roll the *bao* so that it is an even ball shape, then set aside on a well-floured tray and cover with a slightly damp clean cloth or tea towel to keep it from drying out.

Do the same with the rest of the pastries and filling, then allow the uncooked *baos* to rest for a further 30 minutes in a warm, draught-free, humid place, such as a room-temperature oven.

To cook the *baos*, fill a wok one-third to halfway up with boiling water. Line 2 bamboo steam baskets with *dim sum* steamer paper (available online or in specialist shops) or greaseproof paper pierced with holes to let the steam through. Brush the paper with a little vegetable oil, then place the prepared baos in the baskets, twisted side down (to prevent any loose ends from opening up). Put the baskets into the wok, cover with a lid and steam on high for 8 minutes, resisting the temptation to open the lid during this time.

Once steamed, remove the *baos* from the baskets and bring a large frying pan to a medium heat. Add 2 tablespoons of oil and, once hot, carefully place the *baos* in the oil, twisted side down. Once the *baos* have touched the oil, immediately turn them once and fry the other side until golden brown, about 3–4 minutes. Flip and fry the opposite side until golden brown.

Once both sides have been browned nicely, serve piping hot.

TIP: FOR A SIMPLE VEGGIE VERSION OF THIS BAO, OMIT THE BEEF MINCE AND USE A WHOLE EGG IN THE FILLING INSTEAD OF JUST THE YOLK. ONCE THE FILLING INGREDIENTS HAVE BEEN CHOPPED AND MIXED, FRY ON A MEDIUM HEAT IN A WOK OR FRYING PAN AND SCRAMBLE TOGETHER. ALLOW TO COOL, THEN USE AS AN ALTERNATIVE, MEAT-FREE FILLING FOR THE BAOS.

DIM SUM HOUSES

The literal translation of *dim sum*, 'a little touch of heart', stems from this simple, heart-warming story, said to be the origin of the cuisine.

There was once an old lady who owned a tea house along the Silk Road. Tea houses in the old days only served tea, but one day a weary, hungry traveller came to her. It was clear that he had not eaten for days, so the old lady said to him kindly, 'Sit down and have a sip of tea, I'll be right back.'

She popped into the kitchen and found some flour, mixed it with water and oil, gave it a good knead and rolled out thin pastries. She stuffed the little parcels of dough with meat, prawns (shrimp) and finely chopped spring onions (scallions). Worried that her poor guest was wasting away in her front room, she started to steam the dumplings as soon as they had been made, in small batches of 3 or 4, so that he could tuck into them as soon as they came off the steamer, only stopping once all of the dough had been used up. Those basketfuls of dumplings, along with his tea, fuelled the traveller safely home; a little touch of her heart, to him.

Over the years, neighbouring tea houses followed suit, in order to attract customers, each becoming more competitive with its offerings. Though the portions never changed – each plate of dim sum served in threes or fours is there to provide a variety of food to complement the tea – the dumplings became more elaborate in their folds and pleats. Over time the tea houses evolved into what we now know as *dim sum* houses.

If you have ever wondered why some dumplings have such beautifully intricate pleats, the answer

is that *dim sum* is, in essence, a product of the competitive nature of the Chinese culture. The beauty of presentation when it comes to Chinese food isn't about swipes of vibrantly coloured sauces on giant white plates, or even fancy jellies, foams or micro cresses placed just so. Though lovely and deserving of celebration in their own right, they aren't really relevant when it comes to Chinese cuisine. The beauty in our food, especially in *dim sum*, rather than the bold theatrics of many Western presentations, instead stems from the incredibly detailed, finely crafted, subtle skills you might not even notice, required to make those hundreds of tiny pleats and folds. The details of *dim sum* have thus become essential, from the folds to the flavour-balancing, working subtly together to make each morsel rich with a filling so beautifully unique and bursting with vibrancy that each bite becomes impactful and unforgettable, rather than what could easily just be a plain and simple bite of food.

Today, *dim sum* houses can be found all over Hong Kong, from huge harbour-side restaurants all the way down to streetside *dai pai dongs* that serve simple *siu mai* or rice-based *dim sum*. If you want to experience a true example of how much Hong Kongers love the stuff, just wake up at dawn on any given day and head out to see for yourself. Some of the larger *dim sum* houses will be packed full of customers, all having *dim sum* for their breakfast! At that time of day *dim sum* are at their best, the dough and fillings having been freshly made just minutes before they are served. (Although it may also have something to do with the 50 per cent discount they offer before a more reasonable waking hour.)

煲仔、
CLAYPOTS.

麵及炆煮菜式
NOODLES & BRAISES

餐蛋通心粉

MACARONI SOUP WITH SPAM & EGG

The adverse effect that war has anywhere in the world is completely undeniable. Hong Kong in general did not play a huge part in the Second World War; however, after the war, and the multiple change of power and INFLUENCE FROM SEVERAL DIFFERENT COUNTRIES, the people of Hong Kong found themselves sitting between the Americans, the Japanese and the Italians and their WEIRD AND WONDERFUL WAR FOOD CREATIONS: canned meat and dried pasta. In true Hong Kong style and resilience of sorts, this amalgamation of cultures created, among other things, an unlikely fusion of American, Italian NOODLE SOUP, which Hong Kongers now see as a staple: macaroni soup with spam, topped with a fried egg, still available in almost every *cha chaan teng* in Hong Kong as a staple breakfast item on the menu.

SERVES 2

50g (1¾oz) spam
½ a gem lettuce
100g (3½oz) elbow macaroni
2 tablespoons vegetable oil
2 free-range eggs, 1 per bowl
Chiu Chow chilli oil
1 spring onion (scallion), sliced, to garnish
deep-fried shallots, to garnish

THE STOCK

½ a thumb-size piece of ginger
2 spring onions (scallions)
1 clove of roasted garlic, skin on
1 litre (1¾ pints/4 cups) fresh chicken stock
2 tablespoons light soy sauce
1 tablespoon oyster sauce

Finely slice the ginger, and roughly chop the spring onions (scallions). Bash the garlic, skin on. Slice the spam into ½cm (¼ inch) thick batons. Cut the gem lettuce in half lengthways.

Cook the macaroni for 8 minutes, drain and run under cold water to stop the pasta overcooking. Heat 1 tablespoon of vegetable oil in a medium saucepan to a medium heat. Add the ginger, spring onions and garlic. Fry until the garlic and ginger are golden brown, stirring occasionally. Pour in the chicken stock, light soy sauce and oyster sauce and bring to the boil. Reduce the heat to a simmer for 30 minutes. After the soup has been boiling for 30 minutes, add the macaroni and gem lettuce and cook for a further 2 minutes.

Meanwhile, heat the second tablespoon of vegetable oil in a small frying pan to a medium heat. Add the spam and pan-fry until golden brown, then remove from the pan and set aside.

Lastly, return the frying pan back to a medium heat and fry the eggs sunny side up, until the edges of the whites are crispy.

Serve each person a heaped ladle of macaroni in a deep noodle bowl, a scattering of fried spam, topped with a fried egg and spring onions and deep-fried shallots to garnish. Pour 2–3 ladles of soup over the top to finish, and serve with chilli oil for guests to help themselves.

香菇蟹子蒸雞

STEAMED CHICKEN WITH SHIITAKE & ENOKI

SERVES 2

50g (1¾oz) dried shiitake mushrooms
50g (1¾oz) enoki mushrooms
3 skinless, boneless free-range
   chicken thighs
finely chopped spring onions
   (scallions), to garnish

THE MARINADE
½ a thumb-size piece of ginger
a pinch of five-spice
1 tablespoon oyster sauce
½ tablespoon light soy sauce
½ teaspoon sugar
1 teaspoon pure sesame oil
50ml (2fl oz) shiitake soaking water
1 teaspoon cornflour (cornstarch)

Soak the shiitake mushrooms in hot water for at least 2 hours, if not overnight, making sure to save the soaking water for the marinade later. Slice the dry ends off the enoki mushrooms and rinse in cold water.

Cut the chicken thighs into 2cm (¾ inch) dice and put them into a mixing bowl. Finely matchstick the ginger, then add to the bowl with the rest of the marinade ingredients and massage into the chicken. Once the shiitake mushrooms have had time to soak and cool completely, slice them into quarters, then add them to the chicken with the soaking water and the enoki mushrooms and mix well.

Transfer the marinated chicken and mushrooms on to a deep-edged plate or tray suitable for steaming, making sure the plate is small enough to fit into a 26cm (10½ inch) steam basket or directly into a 26cm (10½ inch) wok.

Fill a wok with boiling water to come at least one-third to halfway up the sides. Place the plate of marinated chicken and mushrooms in the steam basket and cover with a lid. Then put the steam basket directly on top of the wok and steam on high (or full boil) for 20 minutes, without the temptation to open the lid at all during this time.

When the chicken and mushrooms are ready, scatter over some finely chopped spring onions (scallions), and serve.

魚香茄子煲

FRAGRANT AUBERGINE (EGGPLANT) WITH MINCED PORK

SERVES 2–4 ALONGSIDE OTHER DISHES

2 Chinese aubergines (eggplants)
1 clove of garlic
1 large fresh red chilli, deseeded (optional, depending on preferred spice level)
½ a thumb-size piece of ginger
a small handful of fresh coriander (cilantro)
100g (3½oz) minced pork (swapsies: 4 finely diced soaked shiitake mushrooms for vegetarians)
400ml (14fl oz/1¾ cups) vegetable oil (or less if pan-frying the aubergines)

THE MARINADE

½ tablespoon oyster sauce
½ tablespoon soy sauce
¼ teaspoon sugar
1 teaspoon pure sesame oil

THE SAUCE

1 tablespoon chilli bean paste
½ tablespoon oyster sauce
200ml (7fl oz/about ¾ cup) chicken stock
1 teaspoon sugar
1 teaspoon Chinkiang black rice vinegar
½ tablespoon Shaoxing rice wine

TIP: IF YOU WOULD RATHER KEEP THIS RECIPE COMPLETELY VEGETARIAN, YOU CAN SIMPLY SWAP OUT THE MINCED PORK WITH FINELY DICED SHIITAKE MUSHROOMS AND SWAP THE OYSTER SAUCE FOR VEGETARIAN STIR-FRY SAUCE.

Leaving the skin on, cut the aubergines (eggplants) in half lengthways. Then cut them into 3–4 cm (1¼–1½ inch) chunks, to end up with approx. 12–16 pieces (depending on the size of your aubergines).

Finely chop the garlic, chilli, ginger and coriander (cilantro), taking care to keep the chilli and coriander separate. Mix all the sauce ingredients together in a bowl. Tip the minced pork into a separate bowl, then add the marinade ingredients and mix well.

Now build your wok clock: place your aubergine pieces at 12 o'clock, then arrange the garlic, ginger, marinated minced pork, chilli, the sauce bowl and lastly the coriander clockwise around the plate.

If deep-frying, put the vegetable oil into a wok and heat to 180°C (350°F), or use a wooden skewer or wooden chopstick to test by placing the tip in the oil: if the wood starts to fizz after a second or two, the oil is hot enough. Carefully add the aubergine pieces and fry for 3 minutes, to immediately seal in their moisture and flavour. Have a metal or ceramic bowl ready with a metal sieve placed on top. Pour the aubergine and oil into the sieve to drain the excess oil, setting the aubergine aside for later.

If you prefer to pan-fry rather than deep-fry, place the aubergine pieces in a mixing bowl and massage well with 1½ tablespoons of oil. Heat a frying pan on a medium heat and cook the aubergine, flesh side down, for 3–4 minutes per side, until both sides are browned. Put into a bowl and set aside for later.

Return the wok to the hob on a medium-high heat. Add the ginger and garlic, immediately followed by the minced pork, and begin to stir-fry, breaking up the meat and browning it well. Bring the wok to a high heat and, once smoking hot, add the sauce and bring to a vigorous boil. Put the aubergine back into the wok and reduce the heat to medium-low, allowing the sauce to simmer and caramelize around the aubergine pieces. Cover with a lid and boil for 8–10 minutes, stirring occasionally.

Scatter over the chopped coriander, and serve.

TIP: WHEN DEEP-FRYING AT HOME, GETTING RID OF OLD OIL CAN BE SLIGHTLY DAUNTING. THE BEST WAY TO THROW AWAY OLD OIL IS TO ALLOW IT TO COOL IN A SAUCEPAN, THEN POUR IT, EITHER THROUGH A FUNNEL OR USING A MEASURING JUG, INTO AN OLD WINE OR OIL BOTTLE. THEN COVER AND THROW IT AWAY. DON'T EVER POUR EXCESS OIL DOWN THE DRAIN.

沙茶醬豉油雞

SOY-POACHED CHICKEN WITH SESAME SHA CHA DIPPING SAUCE

The process of cooking a whole soy-poached chicken is very similar to that of a Hainanese chicken. However, the BEAUTY OF CHINESE COOKING is that simple changes such as caramelizing a mixture of soy sauce and sugar may seem subtle in technique, but make distinct variations in flavour. The SLIGHTLY CARAMELIZED FLAVOUR of the chicken interacts well with the saltiness of the sesame dipping sauce.

SERVES 4–6

1 x 1.5kg (3lb 5oz) whole corn-fed free-range chicken
2 teaspoons salt
1 tablespoon vegetable oil

THE POACHING LIQUID
1 thumb-size piece of ginger
3 spring onions (scallions)
2 tablespoons Shaoxing rice wine
4 tablespoons light soy sauce
3 tablespoons dark soy sauce
2 tablespoons sugar
1 star anise
1 small cinnamon stick
2 cloves
2 litres (3½ pints/8½ cups) fresh chicken stock

THE DIPPING SAUCE
2 tablespoons *sha cha* barbecue sauce
2 tablespoons sesame paste
½ teaspoon white pepper

Remove the parson's nose from the chicken and locate the wishbone with your fingertips – this crossbow-shaped bone is at the top of the breast, surrounding the neck joint. Once you have found it, poke a small paring knife in through either side of the bone and pull it out with your fingers. Then rub the salt all over the skin of the chicken.

Finely slice the ginger and roughly chop the spring onions (scallions). Mix the Shaoxing rice wine, light and dark soy sauces and sugar together in a small bowl.

Heat 1 tablespoon of vegetable oil in a very large saucepan or stockpot on a medium-high heat. Add the sliced ginger and spring onion and stir until the ginger is golden brown and slightly crispy, roughly 30 seconds to 1 minute.

Once the ginger pieces are golden brown, add the star anise, cinnamon stick and cloves and stir for a further minute. Once you start to smell the aroma of the spices, increase to a high heat and add the rice wine, soy and sugar mix. Bring the sauce to a vigorous boil, stir once or twice to melt and caramelize the sugar, then pour the chicken stock into the pan and bring to the boil.

Carefully place the chicken in the pan and top up with hot water from the kettle, so that the chicken is covered completely with liquid.

Put a lid on the pan and simmer on a medium heat for 20 minutes. Now turn off the heat off completely, but keep the chicken in the hot stock for 40 minutes.

Carefully remove the chicken from the pan, reserving the cooking liquid, and submerge the bird in a separate pan of cold water for 2 minutes (this will keep the skin firm and moist). Then remove and set aside to rest for 10 minutes.

Traditionally the chicken is served at room temperature, sliced and jointed, but laid out much like a puzzle, so that it still resembles the whole bird on the plate.

Mix the dipping sauce ingredients together in a small bowl and serve on the side.

煲仔飯類

CLAYPOT RICE VARIATIONS (XO RIBS, AUBERGINE, TOFU & KAI LAN)

The MODERN-DAY FAST FOOD eating culture of Hong Kong does not necessarily lend itself to claypot cooking, since for most Hong Kongers' stomachs and schedules, 20 minutes is just too long to wait for a good meal. When the city is packed to the brim with DELICIOUS AND HIGH-QUALITY 'FAST FOOD', it is too easy to forget that some dishes just need a little time and love. Because of this, there are only a few claypot cafés left in Hong Kong, but they are ABSOLUTELY WORTH EVERY MINUTE of salivating and anticipation while waiting. The beauty of claypot rice cooking, for me, is that the steam from the rice is what gently cooks the marinated meat or vegetables on top, keeping a NATURAL TEXTURE to the food that is to die for.

TIP: IF COOKING THE VEGETARIAN OPTION, TRY PLACING THE KAI LAN OR BROCCOLI INTO THE CLAYPOT RICE FOR THE LAST 5 MINUTES OF COOKING TO AVOID OVERCOOKING.

SERVES 2

EQUIPMENT
a medium-size hob-safe claypot

SETTING UP YOUR CLAYPOT
160g (5¾oz/¾ cup) washed Thai fragrant rice
150ml (5fl oz/⅔ cup) water
3–4 tablespoons vegetable oil

OPTION 1: XO RIBS MARINADE
150g (5oz) pork ribs (chopped by the butcher into small bite-size chunks)
½ a fresh red chilli, finely chopped
2 tablespoons XO sauce
1 tablespoon light soy sauce
½ tablespoon oyster sauce
¼ teaspoon sugar
½ teaspoon pure sesame oil

OPTION 2: AUBERGINE (EGGPLANT), TOFU & *KAI LAN*
½ a Chinese aubergine (eggplant), cut into 3cm (1¼ inch) lengths
3 x 3mm (⅛ inch) thick slices of shop-bought five-spice-pressed tofu
3 stalks of *kai lan*, sliced digaonally (swapsies: tenderstem broccoli)
1 tablespoon vegetarian stir-fry sauce, such as Lee Kum Kee
½ tablespoon hoisin sauce
½ tablespoon light soy sauce
½ teaspoon sugar
½ teaspoon pure sesame oil

Wash the rice well 3 or 4 times, to get rid of as much starch as possible and create a fluffy, rather than sticky, end result. Drain through a sieve.

Depending on which variation you choose for your claypot rice topping, mix all ingredients together, then cover and leave to marinate for a minimum of 1 hour in the fridge.

Put the rice and water into a claypot, then spoon over the marinated meat or vegetables and cover with a lid. Bring the water to the boil on a medium heat, then turn down to a low heat and simmer for 15 minutes, without opening the lid at all.

After 15 minutes, open the lid and spoon 2 tablespoons of the oil all the way around the edge of the claypot, to allow the oil to slip down to the bottom of the pot and around the edge of the rice. Cover once more and continue to cook for a further 3 minutes. Then open the lid and spoon another tablespoon of oil around the edge of the claypot, cover for the final time and cook through for another 3–4 minutes. **Do not be tempted to stir the topping mixture and rice together, as this will affect the cooking success of the dish.**

Lastly, take the claypot off the heat and allow it to sit, covered, for 5 minutes before serving. This last process will allow the rice to fluff up slightly with the excess steam from the meat or vegetables. Serve with a portion of Quick Chilli Soy Sauce (see page 148) on the side.

咖哩牛腩麵

BEEF BRISKET CURRIED NOODLES

SERVES 2

2 small onions
2 cloves of garlic
4 spring onions (scallions)
1 thumb-size piece of ginger
1–2 large fresh red chillies,
    depending on how much heat
    you like
10 fresh curry leaves
300g (10½oz) beef brisket
100g (3½oz) beef tendons
    (if available)
3 tablespoons vegetable oil
1 star anise
1 small stick of cinnamon
2 cloves
2 bay leaves
2 litres (1¾ pints/4 cups) fresh
    chicken stock
200g (7oz) flat egg noodles

THE CURRY PASTE

2 tablespoons Madras curry powder
½ teaspoon chilli powder
½ teaspoon salt
½ tablespoon sugar
6 tablespoons coconut milk
2 tablespoons light soy sauce
1½ tablespoons oyster sauce

Finely dice the onions, then finely chop the garlic, spring onions (scallions) and ginger and place in a bowl. Finely chop the red chillies and set aside with the curry leaves.

Mix all the curry paste ingredients together, then divide between 2 ramekins or small bowls: one for the stock and another to finish the dish.

Cut the beef brisket and beef tendons (if available) into large 2–3cm (¾–1¼ inch) dice. Lastly, boil a kettle full of water, ready to make the stock.

Heat 2 tablespoons of vegetable oil in a large saucepan on a medium-low heat. Add the onions, garlic, spring onions and ginger and fry for 7–8 minutes, until softened and starting to brown, stirring occasionally. Stir in the curry leaves, star anise, cinnamon, cloves, bay leaves and red chillies and allow to cook until you start to smell the fresh aroma of the curry leaves (this should take 30 seconds to a minute). Now add one of the ramekins of curry paste to the pan and stir it in, scraping the base of the pan, continuing on a medium heat until the paste starts to bubble vigorously and stick at the edges.

At this point, immediately add the diced beef to the pan and stir once or twice, coating the meat slightly. Lastly, pour in the chicken stock and bring to the boil, then reduce to a simmer and cook for 2 hours.

Meanwhile, soak the egg noodles in boiling water for 4 minutes until softened, then drain and cool under cold running water. Place on a clean tea towel to dry.

After 2 hours of boiling, the pieces of meat should be soft and tender. Pour everything through a sieve into a large mixing bowl, then pick the meat out of the sieve and put it back into the strained hot stock.

Finally, put the saucepan back on a medium heat and add 1 more tablespoon of vegetable oil. Once hot, add the second ramekin of curry paste and bring to the boil. Then add 3 ladles (roughly 300ml/10fl oz/1¼ cups) of the hot stock from the mixing bowl and bring to the boil once more. Add the soaked noodles and boil for 1 minute.

Once the noodles have soaked up the fragrant sauce from the hot pan, divide between individual bowls, placing a spoonful of meat on each portion, and pouring any extra sauce over the top. Serve with some green vegetables of choice on the side.

車仔麵

CHE ZEI MIEN (LITTLE CART NOODLES)

Over the decades of Chinese immigration to the West, the 'CHINESE BUFFET' has made its mark. Although generally the thought of a Westernized Chinese buffet to me is quite cringe-worthy, I always wonder whether the concept of a buffet like this came from something INCREDIBLY AUTHENTIC, like the olden-day *che zei mien* or little cart noodle stand, which became popular in Hong Kong in the 1950s. The *che zei mien* would have A SELECTION OF SEVERAL BRAISED TOPPINGS, often cooked well in advance, and sometimes consisting purely of leftover ingredients that could not be wasted for fear of profit loss, which were then added to a bowl of noodles of the customer's choice. It was a very popular, and very economical, way of eating something delicious and hot, while also utilizing excess ingredients. Bringing this way of eating into the home, using DELICIOUS, HOME-COOKED LEFTOVERS from your fridge or freezer and turning them into a fun, buffet-like experience, excites me. Here we have less of a recipe and more of a list of suggestions for how to make use of excessive big-freezer food in a FUN AND CREATIVE WAY, which your friends and family will love to get involved with, and won't be able to stop eating (just ask my own, very full, friends and family).

SERVES 8

SUGGESTIONS FOR NOODLES
300g (10½oz) spinach noodles
300g (10½oz) *thin hor fun* (rice noodles)
300g (10½oz) *yau mien* (oil noodles)
300g (10½oz) instant dolly noodles

THE STOCK
½ a thumb-size piece of ginger
2 spring onions (scallions)
3 litres (5¼ pints/12½ cups) fresh chicken stock
2 tablespoons oyster sauce
1 tablespoon light soy sauce
½ teaspoon salt

TO SERVE
1 iceberg lettuce (swapsies: 500g/1lb 2oz *pak choi* or *choi sum*)
3 spring onions (scallions), finely sliced, to garnish

RECIPE LEFTOVERS THAT WILL WORK WITH YOUR HOME-STYLE LITTLE CART (PICK 2–3 OF THESE DISHES)
Red Tofu Braised Pork with Pickled Cabbage & Baby *Pak Choi* (page 114)
Fragrant Aubergine (Eggplant) with Minced Pork (page 80)
Soy-poached Chicken (page 81)
Fish Balls with Curried Dipping Sauce (page 20)
Ham Hock in Yellow Bean Sauce (page 124)
Curried Beef Brisket (page 84)
Any of the wontons or dumplings from the dumplings section
Marbled Tea Eggs (page 24) (leftovers can only be kept in the fridge, cannot be frozen)

Soak the different types of noodles in hot water for 3–8 minutes, depending on thickness, drain well, then dry on a clean tea towel in a mixing bowl or on a baking tray. Run 1 teaspoon of sesame oil through each batch of noodles to keep the strands from sticking together, adding a subtle nutty flavour.

For the stock, bash the ginger with a knife, roughly chop the spring onions (scallions) and put both into a large saucepan with the rest of the stock ingredients. Bring to the boil, reduce the heat and simmer for 30 minutes.

Thinly slice the lettuce and spring onions for garnish. Wash them both well, leaving them soaking in a bowl of cold water for later.

Set up your table with all the ready-soaked noodles, with tongs for serving, and reheat your chosen leftover dishes until piping hot. Bring the stock to the boil and let your dinner companions pick their noodles, adding them to their individual bowls. Blanch each of their noodles individually in the stock for a maximum of 1 minute, then return to their bowl, with a ladle of hot stock. Guests can then help themselves with the rest of the reheated dishes, and sliced lettuce and spring onion to garnish.

To make the experience even more interactive, place the stockpot atop a portable hob in the centre of your table, and let your guests help themselves!

蛋黃蠔油牛柳煲

OYSTER SAUCE BEEF
FILLET & EGG YOLK CLAYPOT

300g (10½oz) beef fillet
1 spring onion (scallion)
½ a thumb-size piece of ginger
3 Chinese garlic sprouts (optional)
  (swapsies: 10 green beans)
1½ tablespoons vegetable oil
1 free-range egg yolk

THE MARINADE
1 tablespoon Shaoxing rice wine
¼ teaspoon sugar
¼ teaspoon salt
½ teaspoon pure sesame oil
a pinch of five-spice
1 teaspoon cornflour (cornstarch)

THE SAUCE
½ tablespoon light soy sauce
2 tablespoons oyster sauce
¼ teaspoon sugar
¼ teaspoon dark soy sauce
50ml (2fl oz) fresh chicken stock

Slice the beef fillet into 3mm (⅛ inch) thick slices and bash once with the side of your knife or cleaver to both thin out and tenderize. Mix the marinade ingredients together in a bowl and massage into the beef slices, then cover and place in the fridge, ideally overnight, or for a minimum of 1 hour.

Cut the spring onion (scallion) diagonally into 2–3cm (¾–1¼inch) lengths and finely matchstick the ginger. Cut the garlic sprouts into 2–3cm (¾–1¼inch) lengths and blanch them in boiling water in the claypot for 3 minutes. Drain in a sieve, then run cold water from the tap over them to stop them overcooking.

Mix the sauce ingredients together in a small bowl.

Heat the vegetable oil to a high heat in a well fired claypot and swirl around the base. Once smoking hot, add the spring onion and ginger and stir for 30 seconds or so, until softened and fragrant.

Layer the slices of marinated beef in the oil and press down on them so that each piece sears well in the oil, then allow them to sit in the hot oil for 1 minute before stirring or moving the ingredients again. After a minute, turn the pieces of beef over to sear the other side, then scatter the blanched garlic sprouts over the top and pour the sauce into the pot, maintaining the high heat for a further 30 seconds. Cover with a lid and remove from the heat.

Just before serving, take off the lid, make a hole in the meat, and carefully lay the egg yolk in the centre. Serve immediately, stirring at the table.

調味粥

CONGEE WITH CONDIMENTS

Every culture has its own cure-alls for flu, colds and other illnesses, alongside HOME REMEDIES and treatments, for children especially. Whether they're soups, or teas, or porridge, these foods all tend to bring COMFORT AND STRENGTH as well as easy digestion – all necessary when battling illness. In Hong Kong, homemade congee may be the only thing that parents will allow their kids to eat when they are suffering any sort of stomach bug, but similarly there is also a huge congee-eating breakfast culture (similar to the UK's porridge culture) that makes for A GREAT START TO THE DAY for adults and kids alike. Here's my aunty Carmen's recipe for a SMOOTH AND SATISFYING congee. For me, much like a simple chip butty, it's the condiments and extras on the side of congee that brings a recipe like this together.

SERVES 4

THE CONGEE
½ a thumb-size piece of ginger
1 spring onion (scallion)
175g (6oz/1 cup) rice
1½ tablespoons vegetable oil
1 teaspoon salt
½ teaspoon white pepper
1 litre (1¾ pints/4 cups) chicken stock
3 litres (5¼ pints/12½ cups) water

THE SOY SAUCE
6 tablespoons light soy sauce
1 teaspoon sugar
2 tablespoons hot water
1 finely sliced seedless bird's-eye chilli

SUGGESTED CONDIMENTS
2 century duck eggs (available in many Chinese supermarkets)
2 tablespoons pickled ginger
2 tablespoons Tianjin preserved cabbage
2 tablespoons deep-fried garlic
2 tablespoons deep-fried shallots
1 finely chopped spring onion (scallion)
3 sprigs of coriander (cilantro), leaves picked

Finely slice the ginger and roughly chop the spring onion (scallion) into 4–5cm (1½–2 inch) lengths. Do not wash the rice, but instead, massage 1½ tablespoons of vegetable oil into the grains and allow the rice to sit, soaking in the oil in a saucepan, for 1 hour. Then add the salt, white pepper, chicken stock and water to the pan, along with the sliced ginger and spring onion.

Place the pan on a high heat and bring to the boil. Once boiling, turn the heat down to the lowest possible setting and, once it's just simmering, cover with a lid. Simmer for 1½ hours, then remove the lid and continue simmering until the congee has started to thicken. At this point, you can serve it as is, or continue boiling until the congee has reached your desired thickness, stirring occasionally so as not to let it stick to the bottom of the pan. My personal preference is to keep it boiling until it has reached a light oatmeal porridge type thickness.

Mix the soy sauce ingredients together in a small bowl or ramekin and serve with the congee, with your choice of condiments on the side.

TIP: TRY THIS RECIPE WITH THE CHINESE SAVOURY DOUGHNUTS RECIPE (OPPOSITE) ON THE SIDE TO DIP INTO THE CONGEE FOR A CLASSIC HONG KONG BREAKFAST.

Pictured overleaf

咸煎餅

CHINESE SAVOURY DOUGHNUT

Note: allow at least one day for preparation.

SERVES 4

extra flour and baking powder, for dusting
1 litre (1¾ pints/4 cups) vegetable oil, for frying, plus extra for oiling the dough

THE DOUGH

500g (1lb 2oz/3¾ cups) medium-gluten wheat flour (swapsies: plain flour/all-purpose flour)
½ teaspoon salt
10g (¼oz) baking powder
50g (1¾oz) salted butter
1 egg
250ml (9fl oz/1 cup) warm water

Put all the dough ingredients into the bowl of an electric mixer fitted with a dough-hook attachment and knead on a low speed for 1–2 minutes. Then turn the speed up to medium and knead for a further 3 minutes, until the dough is smooth. Dust 1 tablespoon of extra flour around the edges of the bowl to help bring the sticky dough off the sides, then tip the dough out on to a lightly floured surface. Knead it lightly with your hands for a minute, then put it back into the bowl and lightly rub it with 1 tablespoon of oil. Cover with a damp cloth and leave to rest for 10–15 minutes.

Dust a 35cm (14 inch) baking tray lightly with flour. After the dough has rested, tip it out on to a floured surface and roll it into a 5mm (¼ inch) thick rectangle, roughly the size of the baking tray. Lay the flattened rectangle of dough on the tray, cover with cling film, then place in the fridge for 8 hours minimum, or overnight.

Now remove the cling film, dust the top of the dough with an additional 5g (⅛oz) of baking powder, and rub it lightly all over the dough. Wet your hands with a little cold water and lightly rub over the dough once more with your wet hands. Using a knife or a dough cutter, cut the dough into roughly 4 x 2cm (1½ x ¾ inch) strips. To make one doughnut, lay one strip directly over another (making sure that the surfaces with the extra baking powder are on the inside of the

dough 'sandwich'), then press down in the centre all along the length of dough with a thin chopstick or the back of a knife to stick the 2 pieces together before frying.

Half-fill a wok or deep-fryer with vegetable oil and heat to 180°C (350°F), or use a wooden skewer or wooden chopstick to test by placing the tip in the oil: if the wood starts to fizz after a second or so, the oil is hot enough.

Pick up the prepared strips and give the ends a light pull away from each other to stretch out the dough, then carefully lay them in the oil and hold them down with tongs or chopsticks so that they puff up as quickly as possible. Gently turn them around in the oil so they cook evenly. The dough sticks should bubble up and become airy very quickly. Deep-fry until golden brown all over. Then remove and drain on a few sheets of kitchen paper. These are traditionally served alongside a bowl of congee for some seriously savoury carb loading.

Pictured overleaf

臘腸鹹蛋煲仔飯

STEAMED RICE POT WITH CHINESE SAUSAGE & SALTED EGG

SERVES 4

FOR 4 CERAMIC OR BONE CHINA RICE BOWLS
80g (2¾oz) rice per bowl
100ml (3½fl oz/⅓ cup) water
   per bowl
a pinch of sugar per bowl
a pinch of salt per bowl
¼ teaspoon vegetable oil per bowl
Chiu Chow chilli oil, to serve
soy sauce, to serve

THE CHICKEN WINGS & WIND-DRIED CHINESE MEATS
1 Chinese sausage
8 whole chicken wings
2 salted eggs (available in Chinese
   supermarkets)

THE MARINADE
1 clove of garlic
1 teaspoon fermented black beans
¼ teaspoon salt
½ teaspoon white pepper
¼ teaspoon sugar
1 tablespoon light soy sauce
1 teaspoon pure sesame oil
1 teaspoon cornflour (cornstarch)

Wash the rice at least 3 or 4 times to get rid of any excess starch. Divide it evenly between 4 small rice bowls and add the stated amount of water to each bowl. Add the sugar, salt and vegetable oil and mix well.

Finely chop the garlic and wash the black beans in cold water. Lightly crush the garlic and black beans together, using either a pestle and mortar or the back of a spoon in a small bowl.

Finely slice the Chinese sausage on an angle, chop the chicken wings into halves or thirds, using a sharp cleaver, and place both in a mixing bowl. Add the black bean mixture and the rest of the marinade ingredients and mix well.

Place 4 pieces of chicken on top of each bowl of rice, along with 6–8 pieces of Chinese sausage. The rice pots are now ready to be steamed.

Fill a wok with boiling water to come at least one-third to halfway up the sides. Put the rice pots into a steam basket and add the 2 salted eggs to the basket whole, without peeling or cracking the shells. Place the steam basket directly on top of the wok, cover with a deep-domed wok lid, and steam on a high heat for 30 minutes, resisting the temptation to open the lid at all during this time.

To serve, slice each salted egg in half and place one half on top of each rice pot. Serve with some Chiu Chow chilli oil and soy sauce on the side.

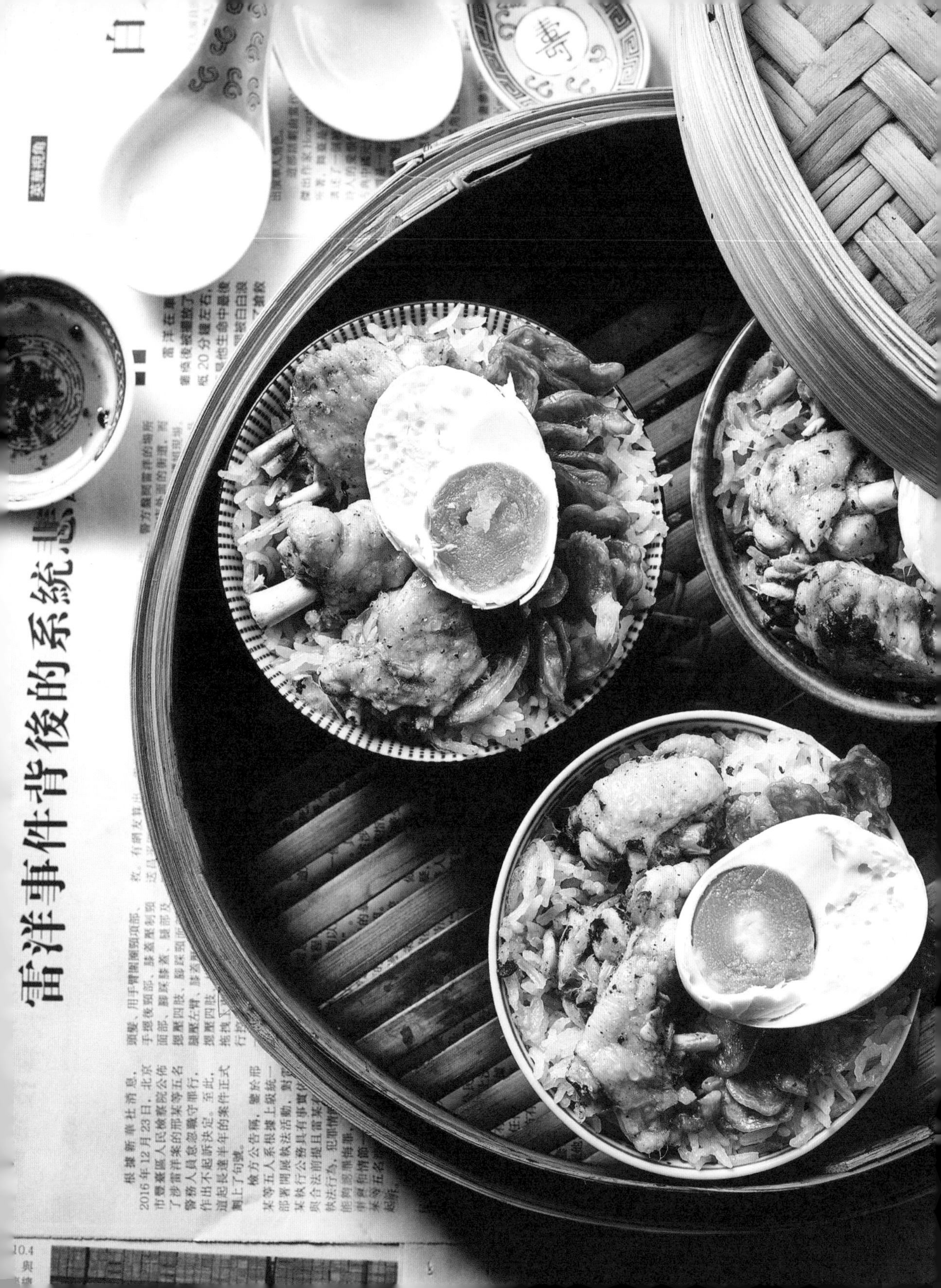
雷洋事件背後的系統

SPECIALIST CAFÉS

Fast food, as we know it here in the UK, has always been the fail-safe option for those who are in need of a quick fix. Often it's pretty nasty or naughty and should be avoided most of the time. But occasionally, after a 12-hour shift on your feet, or a 6-hour shift in the pub, fast food is just what you need, and just has to be obtained and greedily enjoyed. The best thing, I think, about a Hong Kong takeaway or fast food fix, however, is that wherever you go, you are more likely to get a quicker meal from a 50-year-old local establishment than you would queuing up at a big box McDonalds or KFC.

No matter what time of day and how limited your time, your craving for a hearty breakfast, lunch or dinner can be satisfied through an unstoppable and irreplaceable collection of specialist cafés, most of which serve just one or two dishes. Despite the short menu (which might be looked down upon for lack of choice within Western culture), they may well be the very best version of those dishes that you have ever tasted.

If you know where to find them, every district in Hong Kong has its own set of go-to specialist cafés or establishments, serving a plethora of dishes from stuffed fried tofu to claypot rice, traditional steamboats and Hong Kong-style baked breads. As with the *dai pai dongs* (see page 130), it's best not to judge them by their exterior. Some are the most basic of places: essentially just kitchen windows, set up roadside, serving roast duck and pork for takeaway only because there is literally no space to 'eat in' other than the tiny hot kitchen.

A lot of these specialist cafés can still be found in the wet markets or dotted around the outside of them. You'll find these types of eateries spread across the city, wherever locals congregate to do their daily shop, stopping for a quick bite to eat along the way.

My go-to establishments of this genre are the breakfast cafés, where they serve homemade *cheung fun* (steamed rice flour and tapioca pancakes with savoury fillings), rice porridge with a variety of toppings, and stir-fried egg noodles with finely sliced vegetables, with the obligatory chilli sauce on the side for added breakfast kick.

分享套餐

SHARING

港式黑椒牛肉薯仔

BLACK PEPPER BEEF & POTATOES
HONG KONG STYLE

SERVES 3–4

300g (10½oz) rib-eye steak
1 large Maris Piper or King Edward
  potato
1 white sweet potato
1 small red onion
1 spring onion (scallion)
1 large fresh green chilli
1 large fresh red chilli
1 stick of fresh green peppercorns
  (optional)
vegetable oil, for deep-frying
5–6 sprigs of fresh coriander (cilantro)

THE STEAK MARINADE
¼ of a thumb-size piece of ginger
1 clove of garlic
¼ teaspoon white pepper
½ teaspoon sugar
a pinch of salt
½ teaspoon pure sesame oil
½ tablespoon cornflour (cornstarch)

THE SAUCE
¼ teaspoon salt
½ teaspoon sugar
½ teaspoon cracked black pepper
1 tablespoon Lee Kum Kee black
  pepper sauce
50ml (2fl oz) fresh chicken stock
1 tablespoon light soy sauce

Remove any rind or fat from the steak, then slice the meat into roughly 3mm (⅛ inch) thick rectangles. Tenderize by bashing them with a cleaver or meat hammer, creating a large surface area for quick cooking.

Finely chop the ginger and garlic. Place in a bowl, adding the remaining marinade ingredients. Massage the marinade into the meat, then tip into a food bag, seal tightly and marinate in the fridge overnight.

When ready to cook, peel the potato and sweet potato and cut into 2–3cm (¾–1¼ inch) cubes. Put the potatoes into a pan of cold, salted water, and bring to the boil on a high heat. Lower the heat to a simmer and cook for about 5 minutes, until the potatoes start to soften. Drain in a colander, giving the potatoes a little bash around the sides to roughen the edges and allow to cool (do not cover).

Roughly dice the onion and cut the spring onion (scallion) into rough chunks. Roughly chop the red and green chillies. Run your fingers along the stick of the green peppercorns to separate them. Mix the sauce ingredients together in a small bowl.

Now build your wok clock: place the marinated meat at 12 o'clock, followed by the diced onion, spring onion and chillies, and lastly the sauce bowl, clockwise around the plate.

If you have a deep-fat fryer, set the temperature of the oil to 180°C (350°F). Otherwise you can use a wok or large saucepan, filled one-third with vegetable oil, to deep-fry, testing the oil with a wooden chopstick for heat (the end will fizz when the oil is hot enough for deep-frying). Once your oil is hot enough, deep-fry the potatoes for 7–8 minutes, until golden brown and crispy. Then remove from the fryer or wok and drain on a plate covered with kitchen paper.

Heat 5 tablespoons of vegetable oil in a wok on a high heat until smoking hot, then lay the meat in the hot oil, separating each piece as you add it. This is the meat 'blanching' stage – to quickly seal all the flavour and moisture into the meat. Using a slotted spoon or a wok 'spider', fry the meat in the oil for 30 seconds to 1 minute, then remove onto a layer of kitchen paper to soak up the excess oil.

Pour off any remaining oil from the wok into a heatproof bowl and bring to a high heat again. Once smoking hot, add the onion and spring onion and stir-fry for 30 seconds, then add the chillies and fry for 10 seconds. Maintaining a high heat, pour in your sauce, return the meat to the wok and continue to stir-fry for an additional 30 seconds. Add the crispy potatoes, toss through 3 or 4 times to wrap the sauce around them, and tip into a large bowl, ready to serve. Garnish with a few sprigs of coriander (cilantro).

燒鴨

ROAST DUCK

Like most blokes, my attention span when it comes to shopping is incredibly short-lived. In fact WINDOW-SHOPPING is pretty much as far as it goes for me, unless I know exactly what it is I want to buy. In Hong Kong, however, window-shopping is a COMPLETELY DIFFERENT EXPERIENCE. While for some it's handbags a-plenty, for others like myself it's A FEAST FOR THE EYES (and soon afterwards the belly), with ROASTED AND CURED MEATS hanging in just about every third storefront window. Now that's my kind of window-shopping!

WARNING: THIS DISH REQUIRES TIME, PATIENCE AND A BIT OF LOVE (DON'T WE ALL). SO IF YOU'RE PLANNING ON SERVING THIS SHOW-STOPPER FOR YOUR SUNDAY LUNCH, YOU'LL NEED TO BEGIN YOUR PREPARATIONS BY STAYING IN ON SATURDAY NIGHT TO GET STARTED. REST ASSURED, THOUGH, YOUR EFFORTS WILL BE WELL REWARDED.

SERVES 6–8

1 whole duck

THE FILLING
2 star anise
1 small cinnamon stick
2 cloves
10 fennel seeds
1 teaspoon ground ginger
1 teaspoon garlic powder
50ml (2fl oz) Shaoxing rice wine
1 thumb-size piece of ginger
2 spring onions (scallions)

THE GLAZE
4 tablespoons maltose (swapsies: thick honey)
3 tablespoons red rice vinegar (swapsies: red wine vinegar)
2 tablespoons hot water
1 teaspoon salt
½ teaspoon dark soy sauce

Put the star anise, cinnamon stick, cloves and fennel seeds into a dry frying pan over a medium heat and dry fry for 1–2 minutes, until fragrant. Tip the spices into a small bowl, along with the ground ginger and garlic powder and the Shaoxing rice wine. Finely slice the ginger and spring onions (scallions), then add to the bowl and mix together well.

Rub the mixture into and all around the cavity of the duck, leaving any excess bits of fat or skin intact to help close it up. Closing the duck cavity needs a little intuition and resourcefulness. Traditionally, we use a duck needle or meat needle to twist and turn the fat around the cavity until closed. If you do not have such an implement, you can either sew the cavity up with a large needle and some cooking string (butcher's twine) or use a couple of soaked bamboo skewers (soak them in cold water for 30 minutes before using). Most importantly, you want to ensure that the whole spices do not fall out if you are hanging the duck to roast, as the rest of the filling ingredients will get absorbed by the bones and meat eventually while marinating.

Once the cavity has been filled and closed, place the duck, breast side up, on a large metal tray in the sink. Bring a full kettle of water to the boil and pour all of it gradually over the duck. Refill the kettle and bring to the boil once more, turning the duck back side up on the tray, and pour the water over the other side.

Repeat this boiling and pouring on both sides of the duck at least 3 times per side, turning the duck each time. This blanching process will tighten the skin and remove the fatty impurities from the outer layers of the duck skin, eventually creating a crispier finish.

Mix the glaze ingredients together in a jug or mixing bowl, stirring until all the maltose or honey has melted.

Pat the outside of the duck dry with kitchen paper, making sure to get all the way round the skin. Then brush the glaze all over the outside. At this point, the duck will need a few hours to dry out. Traditionally, duck hooks are used to hang the duck in a cool, dry place (I once had a customer dry out a duck in his airing cupboard, although I wouldn't recommend this if your towels are precious to you). The best place to air-dry the duck is either in your oven, hanging off the top shelf with a duck hook, or lying flat on a grill tray in the oven. No matter which way you choose, keep the oven door slightly ajar to allow the air to dry out the skin as much as possible. Hang for a minimum of 6 hours, and a maximum 8 hours before cooking.

For best results and the most even colouring, roast the duck slowly on a barbecue spit, keeping the temperature as close to 160°C (325°F) as possible for 90 minutes to 2 hours, until the skin has a good reddish brown colour. However, if this isn't an option for you, the duck can also be roasted in the oven following the same principle of low and slow. Preheat the oven to 160°C (325°F) and roast for 90 minutes to 2 hours, turning your duck over and around a few times during the process to achieve as even a colouring as possible. No matter which cooking method you choose, baste the duck with the glaze every 15–20 minutes, making sure you brush the glaze all over every part of the skin, in order to get a good colour and, of course, flavour.

Once the duck is cooked, the skin should be a deepish red colour. Don't be put off if your duck doesn't look exactly like the ones you see in restaurants – many tend to favour a bit of help from food colouring to achieve that colour. Remove the duck from the barbecue or oven and allow it to rest for 30 minutes. Then portion the duck into legs, thighs and breast, as you would a chicken. If you're brave enough and you have a good sharp cleaver, chop through the bones carefully with your cleaver to portion it in the more traditional way. Otherwise, just cut it up in the way you feel comfortable with, and let everyone dig in.

香港义燒

HONG KONG CHAR SIU

**SERVES 4–6 IF SERVED
WITH SIDE DISHES**

2 x 300g (10½oz) pieces of pork
neck fillet (swapsies: pork belly
slices for extra fat, or pork fillet for
a leaner finish)

THE MARINADE
½ a thumb-size piece of ginger
2 cloves of garlic
½ teaspoon five-spice
½ teaspoon white pepper
2 teaspoons tomato purée
(tomato paste)
2 teaspoons dark soy sauce
2 tablespoons light soy sauce
2 tablespoons Shaoxing rice wine
4 tablespoons hoisin sauce
2 teaspoons pure sesame oil
4 tablespoons honey

TIP: FOR A QUICK DINNER, YOU CAN ALSO
COOK THIS IN A PREHEATED OVEN AT
200°C/180°C FAN (400°F) FOR 20 MINUTES
ON EITHER SIDE, TURNING ONCE TO CHAR
BOTH SIDES OF THE MEAT AND BASTING
EVERY 10 MINUTES OR SO FOR ADDED
DEPTH OF FLAVOUR.

Finely chop the ginger and garlic,
then mix with all the rest of the
marinade ingredients in a small
bowl. Massage the marinade into
the pork neck fillets, then cover
and put into the fridge to marinate
for at least 1 hour, or overnight for
best results (though this dish can
be cooked immediately if you're
too hungry to wait).

Place the meat on a grill tray,
reserving the marinade for basting.
Preheat the oven to 160°C/140°C
fan (320°F) and roast the pork for
1–1½ hours, until well charred on
the outside, turning once and
basting intermittently with the sauce
to get a good caramelized finish on
the meat. The slower the cooking
process, the more succulent the
meat will become.

If barbecuing instead of roasting,
get your barbecue temperature as
close to 150°C (300°F) as possible
and barbecue for 1–1½ hours, until
well charred on the outside. Baste
as you would in the oven for more
flavour and caramelization.

番茄蔥炒蛋

TOMATO EGG WITH SPRING ONION

Tomatoes are often thought of as a 'WESTERN' INGREDIENT, so it often surprises people visiting a Hong Kong diner when they find tinned tomatoes to be so sought-after. In the busy streets of Central, we happened upon a BUSTLING SIDEWALK CAFÉ, heaving with a hungry crowd impatiently waiting or slurping up their lunch of instant dolly noodles topped with whole, tinned tomatoes. Tomatoes are in fact a HUGE STAPLE of quick Hong Kong cuisine, topping noodles, used in FRESH SMASHED CUCUMBER SALADS, and in this quick comfort dish of eggs, tomatoes and spring onions (scallions), which serves as an EXCELLENT SHARING DISH with a bowl of steamed rice, and possibly one more simple stir-fry, on the side.

SERVES 2–3

1 spring onion (scallion)
1 whole tomato
4 tablespoons vegetable oil

THE EGG MIX
3 free-range eggs
½ tablespoon rice wine or mirin
½ tablespoon light soy sauce
½ teaspoon sugar
¼ teaspoon salt
1 teaspoon pure sesame oil

THE SAUCE
1 tablespoon tomato ketchup
½ teaspoon dark soy sauce
2 tablespoons chicken stock

TIP: THIS DISH WORKS WELL AT ANY MEAL AS A CHEAP, QUICK, RELATIVELY HEALTHY FIX. IT ALSO MAKES A GOOD MEAL ON THE 'DAY AFTER THE NIGHT BEFORE', ALONG WITH A SIDE OF DOLLY NOODLES OR SOME GOOD THICK TOAST OR A CRUSTY ROLL WITH BUTTER.

Whisk the egg mix ingredients together in a bowl. Roughly chop the spring onion (scallion) and cut the tomato into eighths. Mix the sauce ingredients together in a small bowl or ramekin.

Now build your wok clock: place the tomatoes at 12 o'clock, then the egg mix, followed by the spring onion and lastly the sauce.

Bring the vegetable oil to a smoking hot heat in a wok, then add the tomatoes and fold through the oil, so that the skin blisters slightly. Remove the tomatoes with a slotted spoon and put back on top of the spring onions on the wok clock. Now pour half the hot oil from the wok into a small ceramic or metal bowl, so that the finished egg does not come out too greasy.

Heat the wok up once more to a smoking hot temperature. Slowly pour the egg mix into the wok and swirl gently around, keeping the wok on a high heat. Start to fold the egg into itself with a spatula or wok ladle, while continuing to swirl the wok around at the same time. Once the egg is just over halfway cooked and starting to become firmer on the edges but still wobbly, add the tomatoes back in, along with the spring onions. Pour the sauce into the wok, maintaining a high heat for 30 seconds. Toss the wok once or twice, to mix the ingredients and finish cooking the egg, then take off the heat and serve – a truly classic Hong Kong dish.

鹽焗雞

SALT BAKED CHICKEN YIM GUK GAI

SERVES 6

1 x 1.5kg (3lb 5oz) corn-fed
free-range chicken
2 lotus leaves (available in Chinese
supermarkets)
500g (1lb 2oz) rock salt

THE RUB
1 teaspoon mixed cracked black
pepper and sea salt
1 thumb-size piece of ginger
2 spring onions (scallions)
¼ teaspoon five-spice
1 teaspoon ground ginger
2 tablespoons oil

Cut through the back of the chicken and butterfly it by pulling the bones outwards, to open up the bird for a faster cooking time.

Soak the lotus leaves in hot water for at least 30 minutes, to soften and rehydrate them. Cut off the tips of the leaves to make it easier to wrap them round the chicken.

While the lotus leaves are soaking, poach the chicken for 10 minutes in boiling salted water, then carefully remove and place in a large bowl or pot of cold water. Once it has cooled down completely, remove the bird to a cutting board or plate and pat dry with a few sheets of kitchen paper.

For the rub, toast the black pepper and sea salt for 1 minute in a hot dry pan. Finely slice the ginger and slice the spring onions (scallions). Mix all the rub ingredients together in a small bowl, then massage well into the chicken. Cover with cling film and place in the fridge to marinate, for a minimum of 1 hour and ideally overnight.

Place the 2 lotus leaves flush with each other on the work surface and put the chicken on top. Wrap well in the lotus leaves and tie with cooking string (butcher's twine) if necessary, to keep the leaves closed.

Preheat the oven to 220°C/200°C fan (425°F).

Pour all the rock salt into a wok and cover with a lid. Bring the wok to a medium-high heat and warm up the salt for 10 minutes, lifting the lid and turning the salt with a wooden spoon every minute or so, then replacing the lid once again. The salt will make a constant 'crackling' sound throughout the cooking process and will be incredibly hot after 10 minutes in the wok, so be careful when folding and dealing with the hot salt.

Line a large roasting tray with a piece of foil, large enough to wrap the chicken, and pour in half the hot rock salt. Place the wrapped chicken face up on top of the hot salt. Be careful – the salt will be extremely hot! Put on some oven gloves to protect your hands, then cover the chicken with the rest of the hot salt. Wrap the foil carefully around the top of the chicken and place a heavy-based pan on top to weigh the chicken down.

Bake in the oven for 90 minutes. To check that the chicken is fully cooked, carefully unwrap it and poke a small sharp knife through the thickest part of the thigh. If the juices run clear, the chicken is cooked. If more time is needed, bake for a further 10–15 minutes, then check again.

Carefully brush off the salt and leave the chicken to rest for 20 minutes, still wrapped in the lotus leaves. Then unwrap, carve the chicken as you would for a normal roast dinner and serve.

南乳炆豬肉

RED TOFU BRAISED PORK WITH PICKLED CABBAGE & BABY PAK CHOI

SERVES 3–4

THE BRAISED PORK
1 thumbnail-size piece of ginger
½ a spring onion (scallion)
1 tablespoon vegetable oil
400g (14oz) pork belly
500ml (18fl oz/2 cups) fresh
    chicken stock
approx. 500ml (18fl oz/2 cups)
    boiling water
fresh coriander (cilantro) leaves,
    to garnish

THE BRAISING SAUCE
3 tablespoons red fermented tofu
1 tablespoon white fermented tofu
½ tablespoon oyster sauce
1 tablespoon light soy sauce
2 teaspoons dark soy sauce
1 tablespoon sugar

THE STIR-FRIED VEG
1 clove of garlic
½ a thumb-size piece of ginger
½ a spring onion
5 tablespoons Tianjin preserved
    cabbage
10 stalks of baby *pak choi* (swapsies:
    leaves from 3–4 larger *pak choi*)
1 tablespoon vegetable oil

THE STIR-FRY SAUCE
½ tablespoon light soy sauce
100ml (3½fl oz/⅓ cup) chicken stock
½ teaspoon pure sesame oil

Finely slice the ginger, roughly chop the spring onion (scallion), and set aside. Put the red and white fermented tofu into a bowl and mush together with a fork to form a smooth paste. Mix in the rest of the braising sauce ingredients.

Put 1 tablespoon of vegetable oil into a medium, thick-based saucepan, claypot or casserole dish and bring to a medium to high heat. Sear the pork belly, skin side down, until well browned, then repeat on all sides to seal moisture and flavour into the meat. Once all the sides are browned, return it to skin side down in the pan and add the ginger and spring onion and stir well. Once the ginger has browned well, pour the braising sauce ingredients into the pan and bring to a vigorous boil, scraping away anything that sticks to the bottom of the pan and basting the pork with the caramelizing sauce. Baste the pork with sauce for 3–4 minutes, then pour the chicken stock and hot water over the pork to completely cover it. Put a lid on the pan and bring the heat down to medium–low. Simmer for 45 minutes.

After 45 minutes, remove the lid and, using a pair of tongs, remove the pork on to a clean chopping board and slice into 1cm (½ inch) thick slices with a sharp knife. Put the slices back into the simmering braising sauce and continue to

cook, uncovered, for a further 45 minutes, to reduce the sauce. While the pork is slowly cooking, you will have plenty of time to prepare your quick stir-fried vegetable base to the dish as follows. Finely slice the garlic, ginger and spring onion. Wash the Tianjin preserved cabbage in cold water and place in a bowl. Wash the baby *pak choi* or *pak choi* leaves. Mix the stir-fry sauce ingredients in a small bowl or ramekin.

Now build your wok clock for the last-minute stir-fry. Place the ginger, garlic and spring onion at 12 o'clock, followed by the preserved cabbage, then the *pak choi*, and lastly the stir-fry sauce.

Just before serving the dish, bring 1 tablespoon of vegetable oil to high heat in a wok and follow the wok clock order while stir-frying with 30-second intervals between each ingredient. Remember to stir and fold continuously during this cooking process.

To serve, spoon the vegetables into the base of your serving bowl and carefully place the slices of tender braised pork on top. Pour 2–3 ladles of braising sauce over the pork, scatter with coriander (cilantro) leaves, and serve.

豉椒四季豆

DRY-FRIED GREEN BEANS WITH PORK MINCE CHILLI & DARK SOY

Although this dish ORIGINATED IN SICHUAN, it's incredibly popular across China and Hong Kong. Traditionally these dry-fried green beans are DEEP-FRIED FIRST, then stir-fried into a dry mix of pork mince and pickled vegetables. Pickled vegetables are stir-fried into many dishes, and you'll find a few examples in this book. Not only are the pickles DELICIOUS AND FLAVOURFUL, but they also stem from a cultural value of RESOURCEFULNESS by using any and all food available.

SERVES 2

2 large dried red chillies
2 cloves of garlic
50g (1¾oz) *sui mi ya cai* (Sichuanese pickled vegetables) (swapsies: Tianjin preserved vegetable)
200g (7oz) green beans
100g (3½oz) minced pork
200ml (7fl oz/¾ cup) vegetable oil, for frying

THE PORK MARINADE

1 tablespoon light soy sauce
½ teaspoon pure sesame oil
½ teaspoon sugar

THE SAUCE

1 teaspoon chilli bean sauce
½ teaspoon dark soy sauce

Soak the dried red chillies in hot water for 15 minutes, then roughly chop. Keeping all the ingredients separate for now, finely slice the garlic, finely chop the pickled vegetables, and top and tail the green beans.

Mix the pork marinade ingredients together in a bowl, then add the minced pork and massage with the marinade. Lastly, mix the sauce ingredients together in a separate small bowl or ramekin.

Now build your wok clock: place your green beans at 12 o'clock, then arrange the garlic, marinated minced pork, dried red chillies, Sichuan pickled vegetables, and finally the sauce, clockwise around the plate.

Pour the vegetable oil into your wok. This is for deep-frying the green beans. Heat the oil to 180°C (350°F), or use a wooden skewer or wooden chopstick to test by placing the tip in the oil: if the wood starts to fizz after a second or so, the oil is hot enough.

Using a slotted spoon or a Chinese frying skimmer, carefully lay all the green beans in the oil, giving them a gentle push to separate them. The beans will start to blister quite quickly. Deep-fry in the oil for 2 minutes – ideally you want the beans to blister all the way around the skin.

Place a sieve over a metal or ceramic mixing bowl and pour the green beans and oil into the sieve, allowing the bowl to catch the discarded oil.

Place the wok back on a high heat. Once the oil remaining in the wok is smoking hot, add the slices of garlic and stir-fry for 30 seconds, then add the minced pork and chop into it with your ladle or spatula to break up the meat. Once the meat is browning and starting to crisp up on the edges, add the chilli, followed by the pickled vegetables, and cook for a further minute or so, stirring continuously and mixing the ingredients together.

Lastly, return the cooked beans to the stir-fry. Bring the wok to a smoking hot heat one last time, then pour in the sauce and stir-fry for 1 minute. Once all the sauce has coated the meat and beans, the dish is ready to be served, ideally with a side of steamed rice and a steamed vegetable for good balance.

薑蔥蟹

GINGER & SPRING ONION CRAB

Growing up in a family full of dominating, slightly arrogant Chinese cooks made it difficult ever to get a compliment when cooking. The FIRST TIME I EVER EARNED A COMPLIMENT from my dad in the kitchen, was when I cooked this dish, and even then it was so subtly communicated I nearly missed it altogether. The whispered murmurs and NODS OF SATISFACTION around the table stamped the certificate of the highest honour with a waxed seal of approval: MY FIRST EVER CULINARY ACHIEVEMENT, handed down by the most scrupulous of judges. Recently, while in Hong Kong, I had the honour of working with true wok master Sing Gor (big brother Sing) at his *dai pai dong*. And wouldn't you know, the one dish he picked off his menu for me to make was this exact recipe. The significance for me was just as delicious as the dish itself.

SERVES 2–3

½ a small red onion
2 spring onions (scallions)
1 thumb-size piece of ginger
1 medium live mud crab
vegetable oil, for frying

THE SAUCE
1 tablespoon light soy sauce
1 tablespoon oyster sauce
½ tablespoon Shaoxing rice wine
¼ teaspoon salt
1 teaspoon sugar
150ml (5fl oz/⅔ cup) chicken stock

Dice the red onion into 1cm (½ inch) chunks, then roughly chop the spring onions (scallions) and finely slice the ginger. Mix the sauce ingredients in a bowl.

A word of warning: crab is best eaten when prepared from live. There are plenty of wonderfully detailed videos which will help you when deciding to kill the crab yourself (even one from myself – just google it!).

However, if you are uncomfortable killing the crab yourself, I suggest using a ready-boiled crab with the shell on. The method below assumes your fresh crab is no longer alive.

To portion the crab, first carefully remove the claws, using a quick twist. Then, keeping the crab on its back, place your fingers underneath the legs, between the body and the underside of the legs, and place your 2 thumbs pointing firmly upwards towards the legs. Push your thumbs firmly upwards, while pushing your fingers down towards the body and the table. You may find that running a blunt knife around the small gap between the shell and the legs will help to loosen the shell at this stage. This will help to separate the body from the legs.

Once you have separated the two parts, remove and discard the brown 'fingers' which are on top of the inside part of the legs, as these are not edible. Place the head shell to one side in a bowl

and clean the chopping board, ready to portion the rest of the crab. Chop the leg parts into quarters and bash them lightly with the side of your cleaver to loosen the shell, then place in a large mixing bowl. Crack the claws with the side of your cleaver, again to loosen the shell, and place in the mixing bowl.

Lastly, add 1½ tablespoons of cornflour (cornstarch) to the bowl, cover with a plate or lid, and give the whole bowl a shake, to coat the pieces of crab.

Half-fill a medium pot, wok or deep-fryer with vegetable oil and heat to 180°C (350°F), or use a wooden skewer or wooden chopstick to test by placing the tip in the oil: if the wood starts to fizz after a second or so, the oil is hot enough.

Using a slotted spoon or a Chinese frying skimmer, carefully lay the pieces of crab in the hot oil and deep-fry for 3–4 minutes. Remove the crab and place on a couple of pieces of kitchen paper to drain off any excess oil. If you have been using a wok, pour the deep-frying oil into a metal or ceramic mixing bowl.

Heat 1 tablespoon of vegetable oil in the wok to a high heat and when smoking hot, add the onions, ginger and spring onion. Stir-fry for 1 minute on a high heat, then add the crab portions and stir-fry for a further 2 minutes. Now stop stirring the crab completely, to allow the wok to heat up as much as possible and become smoking hot. Pour in the sauce, cover with a lid and leave for 1 minute, still on the heat.

Remove the lid and stir through once or twice, then serve. It's best when eaten with your fingers, a cold beer and a pile of napkins or wipes on hand for cleaning up.

TIP: IF USING LIVE CRAB, KEEP THE CRAB IN THE COLDEST PART OF YOUR FRIDGE, AS THEY BECOME DORMANT IN COLD TEMPERATURES AND WILL THEREFORE BE EASIER TO HANDLE.

煎鯧魚

CRISPY POMFRET WITH SWEETENED SOY

SERVES 2–3

½ a thumb-size piece of ginger
1 spring onion (scallion)
1 x 400g (14oz) whole pomfret,
 scaled and gutted (swapsies:
 small flounder or lemon sole)
6 tablespoons cornflour (cornstarch),
 mixed with ½ teaspoon black
 pepper and ½ teaspoon salt
10 tablespoons vegetable oil, for
 shallow-frying

THE SAUCE
4 tablespoons light soy sauce
2 tablespoons sugar
6 tablespoons hot water

Finely matchstick the ginger and spring onion (scallion) and set aside separately. Mix the sauce ingredients together in a small bowl or ramekin and stir until the sugar is fully dissolved.

With the pomfret lying horizontally on a board, cut 3 or 4 vertical slits into the side of the fish, pushing the tip of the knife down just until you reach the bone, without slicing all the way through. Rub the chopped ginger all over the fish, followed by the seasoned cornflour (cornstarch). Take special care to coat the fins and tail with cornflour, to make sure everything is dry and ready for frying.

In a large frying pan big enough to fit the whole fish, heat the oil to a high heat. Once the oil is smoking hot, lay the fish carefully in the frying pan and press down with a spatula to ensure every part touches the hot oil. Turn the heat down to medium-low and fry for 4–5 minutes, to cook the fish through without burning. Then turn the heat back up to high, turn the fish over and repeat the process on the other side; press down to crisp up the other side, then turn the heat down to medium-low and fry for a further 4–5 minutes.

Once cooked, you should see that the slits in the fish will have opened up slightly, and the flesh inside should be whitish in colour and completely opaque.

Remove the fish from the pan and place it on a couple of sheets of kitchen paper to drain any excess oil. Put the fish on a serving plate, and scatter the fine matchsticks of spring onion all over. Heat up the oil remaining in the frying pan to a high heat. Once smoking hot, pour a little of the oil over the sliced spring onion, then pour a few tablespoons of the sauce over the fish and serve.

臘味炒芥蘭

KAI LAN, CHINESE SAUSAGE & WIND DRIED HAM WITH GINGER & SPRING ONION (SCALLION)

DRIED AND CURED MEATS play a big part in flavouring stir-fries and claypot cooking in Hong Kong cuisine, and can easily be found in Chinese supermarkets.

SERVES 2–3

½ a thumb-size piece of ginger
1 clove of garlic
1 spring onion (scallion)
10 stalks of *kai lan*
1 Chinese sausage
½ a piece of Chinese cured pork belly
   (swapsie: wind-dried Ibérico pork)
1 tablespoon vegetable oil

THE SAUCE
1 tablespoon yellow bean sauce
1 tablespoon light soy sauce
1 tablespoon Shaoxing rice wine
¼ teaspoon dark soy sauce
50ml (2fl oz) chicken stock
a pinch of salt
½ teaspoon sugar

Finely slice the ginger and garlic and roughly chop the spring onion (scallion). Slice the *kai lan* diagonally lengthways and set aside. Slice the Chinese sausage into diagonal slices similar to the *kai lan*, and thinly slice the cured pork. Mix all the sauce ingredients together in a small bowl.

Now build your wok clock: place the finely sliced ginger and garlic at 12 o'clock, followed by the spring onion, then the slices of cured pork, Chinese sausage, *kai lan* and lastly the bowl of sauce, clockwise around the plate.

Bring 1 tablespoon of vegetable oil to a high heat in a wok and swirl around to coat the whole of the inside. Once smoking hot, add the ginger, garlic and spring onion and stir-fry for 30 seconds. Add the cured pork belly and Chinese sausage, then turn the heat down to medium so as not to burn the meat. Stir-fry for another minute or so, or until you start to smell the sweet aroma of the Chinese sausage.

At this point, turn the heat up once more, add the *kai lan* and stir-fry for a further minute, then pour the sauce into the wok, bring to a vigorous boil and continue to stir-fry for a further 2 minutes. Once the centre of the *kai lan* pieces has turned a dull green colour, the stir-fry is ready.

Best served with a bowl of steamed rice on the side and a nice slow-braised claypot dish if you're feeling really hungry.

菜心拌特製魷魚餅

HOMEMADE SQUID FISH CAKES WITH CHOI SUM

SERVES 2–3

THE FISH CAKES
150g (5oz) skinless dace fillet
   (swapsies: coley or any white
   river fish)
50g (1¾oz) cleaned squid tubes
1 clove of garlic
¼ teaspoon salt
¼ teaspoon white pepper
1 teaspoon pure sesame oil
1 tablespoon cornflour (cornstarch)
1 spring onion (scallion)
3 sprigs of fresh coriander (cilantro)
4 tablespoons vegetable oil, to cook
   the fish cakes

THE STIR-FRY
½ a thumb-size piece of ginger
300g (10½oz) *choi sum*

THE SAUCE
150ml (5fl oz/⅔ cup) fresh
   chicken stock
1 tablespoon oyster sauce
½ tablespoon light soy sauce
¼ teaspoon salt
¼ teaspoon sugar

Dab the fish fillet and squid tubes dry with kitchen paper, then roughly chop and place in a food processor. Finely chop the garlic and add to the processor with the salt, white pepper, sesame oil and cornflour (cornstarch), then pulse until a completely smooth paste has formed. I find it helps to stop once in order to check for any large clumps and separate them out.

Finely chop the spring onion (scallion) and roughly chop the coriander (cilantro), then fold both into the paste with a wooden spoon. Using a dessertspoon dipped in cold water, scoop out spoonfuls of the fish mixture and shape them into individual round fish cakes, placing them carefully on a large clean plate, ready to fry.

Finely slice the ginger for the stir-fry and set aside, then roughly chop the *choi sum* into 3cm (1¼ inch) lengths. In a jug or bowl, mix together all the sauce ingredients.

Now build your wok clock: place the ginger at 12 o'clock, then the chopped *choi sum* and lastly the sauce.

Heat 4 tablespoons of vegetable oil in a wok to a medium-high heat, swirling it around to ensure that the whole wok is non-stick. Once the oil is smoking hot, put the fish cakes into the wok and fry for 1 minute on each side, or until golden brown. Place a sieve on top of a metal or ceramic mixing bowl and very carefully transfer the fish cakes and oil into the sieve, draining the oil into the bowl and setting the fish cakes aside.

Put the wok straight back on the hob on a high heat. Now add the slices of ginger and stir-fry quickly until golden brown. Add the *choi sum* and toss through once or twice, then, keeping the wok on a high heat, pour in the sauce. Put the fish cakes back into the wok on top of the *choi sum* and cover everything with a lid. Bring the sauce to the boil and cook for 2 minutes, stirring occasionally, then serve immediately, with a side of steamed jasmine rice to absorb any additional sauce.

豉椒蟶子

RAZOR CLAMS WITH BLACK BEAN CHILLI

SERVES 3–4

2 cloves of garlic
½ a thumb-size piece of ginger
2 teaspoons preserved fermented
  black beans
1 fresh red chilli
1 spring onion (scallion)
12 fresh razor clams (swapsies:
  500g/1lb 2oz fresh mussels)
vegetable oil, for frying
fresh coriander (cilantro) leaves,
  to garnish

THE SAUCE
1 tablespoon light soy sauce
½ tablespoon oyster sauce
½ tablespoon hoisin sauce
1 tablespoon Shaoxing rice wine
100ml (3½fl oz/⅓ cup) chicken stock
1 teaspoon sugar

Finely chop the garlic and ginger, then ideally put into a mortar, or alternatively a food processor. Wash the fermented black beans, and add to the mortar or food processor and crush together to form a paste. Finely chop the red chilli and spring onion (scallion), keeping them separate. Combine all the sauce ingredients in a small bowl or ramekin.

Soak the razor clams in salted cold water for 10 minutes, then blanch in boiling hot water for 1 minute. Once they have cooled so they can be handled, they need to be cleaned. Much like mussels, in razor clams there is a 'beard' of sorts that can be quite dirty. The clams should have opened up from the blanching process, and you will now see the white meat, with a slightly dark part attached to the meat. Pull apart and discard the dark, sandy part of the clam until you are left with just the white meaty parts of the clams, while continuing to clean each shell under the running cold tap. Once the clams have been cleaned thoroughly, place them in a bowl of cold water once more.

Now build your wok clock:
place the razor clams at 12 o'clock, then arrange the spring onions, black bean paste, chilli and lastly the sauce bowl clockwise around the plate.

Bring 1 tablespoon of vegetable oil in a wok to a high heat and swirl it round the wok with your ladle or spatula. Once smoking hot, add the spring onion and stir-fry for 30 seconds. Next add the black bean paste and fry for a further 10–20 seconds.

Add 1 teaspoon of vegetable oil to the wok and allow it to smoke. Add the chilli, stir-fry continuously for 10 seconds, then pour in the sauce. Bring to a vigorous boil, then add the clams, folding the sauce evenly through them, and cover with a lid. Steam with the lid on for 1 minute, then remove the lid and fold everything together once more for a final minute or two to make sure it's all evenly coated and seasoned.

Serve immediately, garnished with the coriander (cilantro) leaves and a few of the blanched razor clam shells.

五香元蹄

SLOW BRAISED HAM HOCK IN YELLOW BEAN SAUCE, WHITE PEPPER & FIVE-SPICE

Anything pork GOES DOWN A STORM in Hong Kong. Traditionally this dish can be found during the winter at *dai pai dongs* (see page 130). Its hearty slow-cooked process makes a perfect main dish for serving with a few others: crispy squid with chilli and garlic, or sweet and sour whole prawns (shrimp), along with a stir-fried vegetable and some steamed rice on the side for a TRULY BALANCED FEAST.

SERVES 5–6

1 red onion
½ a leek
1 teaspoon salt
½ teaspoon white pepper
¼ teaspoon five-spice
1kg (2lb 4oz) ham hock on the bone, with skin on
2 tablespoons whole black peppercorns
1 bay leaf
1 star anise
1 cinnamon stick
2 tablespoons vegetable oil
500ml (18fl oz/2 cups) chicken stock
500ml–1 litre (18fl oz–1¾ pints/ 2–4 cups) hot water
2 teaspoons cornflour (cornstarch), mixed with 3 tablespoons water

THE BRAISING SAUCE

3 tablespoons Chingkiang black rice vinegar
2 tablespoons sugar
3 tablespoons yellow bean sauce
2 tablespoons light soy sauce
1 tablespoon dark soy sauce

Cut the red onion into roughly 2cm (¾ inch) chunks and halve the leek lengthways. Wash the leek well under cold running water and cut into 3cm (1¼ inch) lengths. Mix all the braising sauce ingredients together in a small bowl.

Rub the salt, white pepper and five-spice all over the ham hock and set aside on a roasting tray.

Now build your wok clock: place the red onion at 12 o'clock, followed by the leeks, the black peppercorns, bay leaf, star anise and cinnamon stick, then the braising sauce, clockwise on the plate.

Heat 1 tablespoon vegetable oil to a medium-high heat in a large saucepan. Once hot, place the ham hock skin side down in the pan and turn it until completely seared all over – about 5–8 minutes in total. Add the red onion around the edge of the ham and fry for a further minute or so, then add the leeks, peppercorns and bay leaf, giving them a quick stir for another minute or two.

Turn the heat up to high, then pour the braising sauce into the pan and bring to a vigorous boil. Turn the ham hock every minute or so, coating all sides in the boiling sauce. The sauce will begin to reduce and thicken, starting to stick a little on the base of the pan. At this point, pour in the chicken stock and hot water to cover the ham hock completely, and return to the boil.

Give it a stir to mix all the flavours together, then turn the heat down to medium-low and leave to cook for 1½ hours.

After about 1 hour of braising the meat, preheat the oven to 220°C/200°C fan (400°F). Once the meat has had its 1½ hours of braising, transfer the ham hock to a roasting tray.

Heat 1 tablespoon of oil in a wok to a high heat. Scoop out all the red onions and leeks from the braising liquid, add them to the wok and fry for 30 seconds, then immediately add 4–5 ladles of braising liquid and bring to a vigorous boil.

Add the cornflour (cornstarch) paste, return to the boil and stir continuously for 1 minute more. Once the sauce has thickened slightly, pour it directly over the ham hock, then place the roasting tray in the oven for a further 20–30 minutes.

This is a great dish for everyone to get stuck in, pulling pieces apart as they go.

粵式豬扒

CANTONESE PORK CHOPS

WORCESTERSHIRE SAUCE, brown sauce and ketchup are a true show of how British food has been intertwined into Hong Kong cuisine. UNUSUAL INGREDIENTS to find in typical 'Chinese food' perhaps, yet when combined with chilli oil and soy sauce, the BALANCE OF sweet and sour flavours marries seamlessly, creating the same flavour balance that Cantonese cuisine is so famous for.

SERVES 4

4 x 200–250g (7–9oz) pork chops
1 red onion
vegetable oil, for frying
fresh coriander (cilantro) leaves,
   to garnish

THE MARINADE
2 cloves of garlic
½ a thumb-size piece of ginger
1 spring onion (scallion)
1 teaspoon sugar
½ teaspoon salt
¼ teaspoon white pepper
1 teaspoon pure sesame oil
1 tablespoon Shaoxing rice wine
1 tablespoon light soy sauce
2 tablespoons cornflour (cornstarch)

THE SAUCE
1½ tablespoons dark soy sauce
3 tablespoons Worcestershire sauce
3 tablespoons tomato ketchup
4½ tablespoons Chingkiang black
   rice vinegar
4½ tablespoons sugar
1½ teaspoons Chiu Chow chilli oil

Slice the pork chop meat off each bone in one long sweep, keeping each chop as one whole piece of meat and reserving the bones, as they are great to cook too.

Turn your cleaver upside down and, using the blunt end (careful not to hold the blade!), bash across the meat as many times as possible to flatten it out, making indentations along the pork and creating as much of a surface area as possible. This will begin to tenderize the chop and allow the marinade to really flavour the meat. Keep each pork chop in one large piece at this stage.

Once the pork is flattened, a similar thickness to an escalope, mix the marinade ingredients in a bowl and massage them into the bashed-out meat and the bones until they are completely coated. Leave to marinate in the fridge, ideally overnight, and for a minimum of 1 hour.

When ready to make the dish, finely slice the red onion and set aside. Mix the sauce ingredients together in a bowl and stir well until the sugar has fully dissolved.

Half-fill a medium pot, wok or deep-fryer with vegetable oil and heat to 180°C (350°F), or use a wooden skewer or wooden chopstick to test by placing the tip in the oil: if the wood starts to fizz after a second or so, the oil is hot enough. Using a slotted spoon or a Chinese frying skimmer, first

lay the marinated pork chop bones in the oil and deep-fry them for 5 minutes. Remove the bones and drain well on kitchen paper, then lay the marinated pieces of pork in the fryer one by one, so they don't stick together. Deep-fry the pork for 2–3 minutes on a high heat, until crispy and brown on the outside, then remove and drain with the bones.

At this point, roughly chop the fried pork meat into bite-size portions (roughly 3cm/1¼ inch squares).

Heat 1 tablespoon of vegetable oil in a wok to a high heat. Once smoking hot, add the finely sliced red onion and stir-fry for 30 seconds or so. Pour in the sauce and bring to a vigorous boil, then add the bones and the pieces of fried pork meat and toss 2 or 3 times. Serve immediately, garnished with coriander (cilantro) leaves.

琵琶豆腐

PEI PA DOU FU – QUENELLE FRIED TOFU

Also known as 'PEAR-SHAPED TOFU', this dish is often cooked in restaurants using a mixture of prawns (shrimp) and tofu. This version, however, is just as good without the prawns, fully vegetarian if desired. The whole salted egg adds a little texture and flavour to the tofu quenelles.

SERVES 4

½ a thumb-size piece of ginger
1 spring onion (scallion)
3 whole *pak choi*
1 tablespoon cornflour (cornstarch)
3 tablespoons water
vegetable oil, for frying

THE TOFU MIX
4 dried shiitake mushrooms
1 whole steamed salted egg
500g (1lb 2oz) fresh firm tofu
2 cloves of garlic
¼ of a thumb-size piece of ginger
1 spring onion (scallion)
6 whole green beans
¼ teaspoon salt
¼ teaspoon white pepper
1 teaspoon pure sesame oil
3 tablespoons cornflour (cornstarch)
1 egg yolk

THE SAUCE
1½ tablespoons Lee Kum Kee vegetarian stir-fry sauce (swapsies: oyster sauce)
½ tablespoon light soy sauce
3 drops of dark soy sauce
300ml (10fl oz/1¼ cups) mushroom soaking water (see method)

Soak the shiitake mushrooms in hot water for a minimum of 2 hours, or ideally overnight, then drain, reserving the soaking water. Finely slice the ginger and roughly chop the spring onion (scallion). Slice the *pak choi* into quarters, lengthways.

Boil the salted egg for 10 minutes, then peel and mash with a fork. Press the fresh tofu for 10–15 minutes by placing a couple of pieces of kitchen paper on a large plate, followed by the tofu, topped with a couple more sheets of kitchen paper and another large plate.

Finely chop the soaked mushrooms, garlic, ginger and spring onion and place in a large mixing bowl. Top and tail the green beans and finely chop. Dry the tofu by dabbing it well all over with kitchen paper, then put it into a mixing bowl with the beans and all the remaining tofu mix ingredients apart from the cornflour (cornstarch) and egg yolk. Use your fingertips to break the tofu up, creating a thick paste. Add the cornflour and egg yolk, mix well and set aside.

Mix the sauce ingredients together in a bowl. Lastly, mix 1 tablespoon of cornflour and 3 tablespoons of water to make a paste.

Half-fill a medium pot, wok or deep-fryer with vegetable oil and heat to 180°C (350°F), or use a wooden skewer or wooden chopstick to test by placing the tip into the oil: if the wood starts to fizz after a second or so, the oil is hot enough.

Using 2 dessertspoons, carefully 'quenelle' the tofu, then lay a quenelle of tofu mix in the hot oil. Fry in batches of 5 or 6 at a time, keeping the oil at a high temperature, until golden brown all over, roughly 3–4 minutes, then remove from the hot oil with a slotted spoon or a Chinese frying skimmer and drain on kitchen paper. Repeat until all your tofu mixture has been used up.

Now heat 1 tablespoon of vegetable oil in a medium saucepan or claypot to a medium-high heat. Add the sliced ginger and roughly chopped spring onion and stir through for 30–60 seconds. Pour the sauce into the pan and bring to the boil, then add the *pak choi* and cook in the sauce for 2 minutes.

Place the *pak choi* in a serving dish. Stir the cornflour paste into the sauce and bring to the boil. Add the fried tofu pieces to the pan and continue boiling for 1–2 minutes, carefully coating the tofu quenelles with the sauce. Pour the tofu and sauce over the *pak choi* and serve.

TIP: IF YOU FRY THE TOFU 'QUENELLES' WITH A LITTLE PATIENCE (I DEEP-FRY NO MORE THAN 5 OR 6 PIECES AT A TIME, TO PREVENT TOO MUCH COOLING OF THE OIL AND STOP THE PIECES STICKING TOGETHER), EACH MORSEL OF MIXED TOFU WILL COME OUT SEPARATE, NICE AND CRISPY. IN OTHER WORDS, FRY PATIENTLY TO AVOID THE WHOLE DISH GOING PEAR-SHAPED!

If you've ever watched a Hong Kong gangster movie, or even just an 'old school' martial arts movie, you'll know what a *dai pai dong* is, even if you've never been to Hong Kong. At the start of the movie, once the cameras have finished panning across the bird's-eye view of the skyscrapers and twinkling harbours, the real action begins, most often in the middle of a crowded street market. Once they hit the market scene there is likely to be a token shot of some guy in a sweat-stained white tank top, wielding a giant cleaver or whisking a featherweight wok. THAT is a *dai pai dong*. Bare-boned, streetside, run by one or two people with equal amounts of equipment. That is the real deal.

This type of street food eating establishment has been around in Hong Kong since the 1800s, although at that time they were completely unlicensed. After the Second World War the colonial Hong Kong government issued ad hoc licences to families of deceased and injured civil servants, allowing them to operate food stalls in public and thereby earn a living. It was part of the licensing law that every owner of such a stall must display a photo of the licence on the stall itself and so, as we have such a literal culture, the locals named the operation *dai pai dong* (big licence stall).

These *dai pai dongs* or 'big licence stalls' are where I would send someone for the most street-level, fully immersive, sink-or-swim experience if asked to give someone the most authentic lesson in Cantonese cooking. It's been a dream of mine to get a lesson in '*wok-hei*' from the true street chefs of Hong Kong since I was a kid. I have deep respect for all chefs, from those who have worked hard to make their way to the very top and now have accolades and stars to show for it, to those peeling potatoes with diligence or performing other back-breaking yet vital tasks within the food industry. To me personally, however, none can hold a candle to the fierce owner of a *dai pai dong*, flicking a huge wok around a 32-jet-point wok burner rigged up on a portable gas canister, then just a minute later serving up the most succulent, crispy, slightly smoky sweet and sour pork you've ever tasted. Those are the guys with grit, and the true alchemists, not to mention performers of the industry.

Dai pai dongs are, unfortunately, a dying trade in Hong Kong, with only a scarce fifteen establishments left, due both to the legal logistics of taking over their licences and to the surge of hawker centres and air-conditioned eateries. But if you ask me, they are the culmination point of Hong Kong street food culture, and should not be missed if you are ever presented with the opportunity to visit one of them.

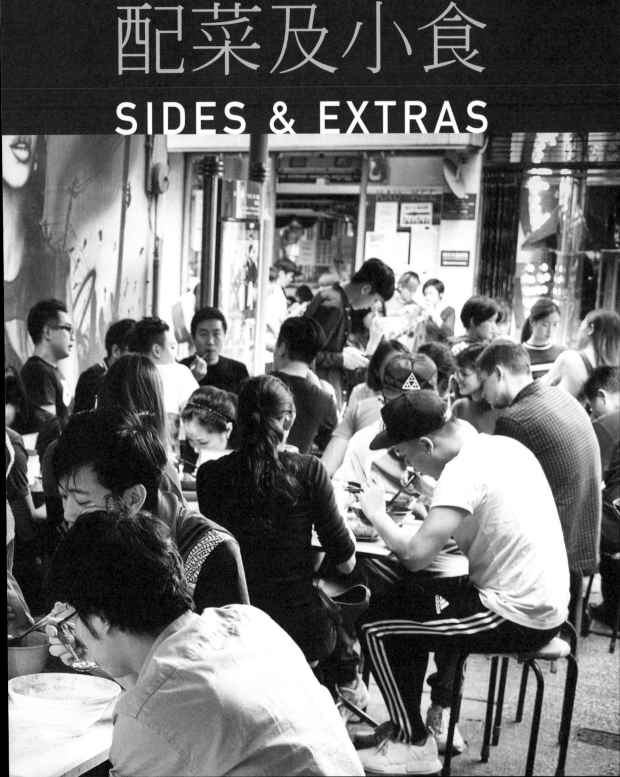

配菜及小食

SIDES & EXTRAS

青瓜木耳沙律

CUCUMBER & WOOD EAR FUNGUS SALAD WITH TOBAN JIANG & CRUSHED SOY BEANS

10g (¼oz) dried wood ear fungus
½ a cucumber
½ a spring onion (scallion)
5 sprigs of fresh coriander (cilantro)
½ teaspoon pure sesame oil
a pinch of salt

THE DRESSING
1 clove of garlic
½ a spring onion
2 tablespoons *toban jiang* chilli
  bean sauce
1 tablespoon light soy sauce
1 teaspoon sugar
2 teaspoons rice vinegar
1 teaspoon Chiu Chow chilli oil
2 tablespoons soaking water from the
  wood ear fungus

Soak the wood ear fungus in hot water for a minimum of 1 hour. Slice the cucumber lengthways into quarters, keeping the seeds in, then cut into 5mm (¼ inch) chunks. Finely chop the white part of the spring onion (scallion) to use in the dressing, and cut the greens into fine rings for garnishing later. Pick the coriander (cilantro) leaves and place in a serving bowl with the cucumber.

Drain the soaked wood ear fungus in a sieve over a mixing bowl (to save the soaking water) and add the fungus to the cucumber, seasoning with the sesame oil and a pinch of salt.

Finely chop the garlic and mix well with the rest of the dressing ingredients until the sugar has dissolved. Pour the dressing over the seasoned cucumber and wood ear fungus, and serve garnished with the spring onion greens.

美珍小炒

LEFTOVER STIR-FRY — MEI CHUM SIU CHOW

Hong Kongers place great emphasis on creating as LITTLE WASTE AS POSSIBLE when it comes to cooking. And while this flags up concepts such as sustainability, I think this waste-free culture is more about our undying LOVE FOR ALL THINGS EDIBLE. Wasted food, after all, means something delicious will end up somewhere else, other than in our stomachs – a punishment in and of itself which perma-hungry people like myself are keen to avoid. Here in the UK, the issues surrounding food waste are finally starting to come into the spotlight on a national scale. But no matter what the agenda – whether it's people in need or depleting resources that you wish to focus on – I have found that keeping a waste-free mentality can truly work as inspiration to make for A GREAT MEAL. A simple example: recently while at a *dai pai dong* (see page 130) in Hong Kong, one of the best dishes we tried was actually called a 'leftover stir-fry' on the menu, which changed every day, depending on what needed to be cooked so it didn't go to waste. Literally translated from *mei chum siu chow* to mean 'beautiful delicacy small stir-fry', it certainly feels like A THING OF BEAUTY to use every last bit of available food, turning it from something ordinary into a delicacy worth writing about.

SERVES 3–4

1 tablespoon dried shrimps
2 cloves of garlic
1 large fresh red chilli
1 stalk of pickled *pak choi*
300g (10½oz) Chinese garlic sprouts (swapsies: wild garlic or garlic shoots)
100g (3½oz) cleaned baby squid
½ tablespoon cornflour (cornstarch)
1½ tablespoons vegetable oil

THE SAUCE

1 teaspoon chilli bean sauce
1 teaspoon rice vinegar
1 teaspoon sugar
1 tablespoon light soy sauce
½ tablespoon oyster sauce
½ tablespoon hoisin sauce
100ml (3½fl oz/⅓ cup) vegetable stock
1 teaspoon pure sesame oil

Soak the dried shrimps in hot water for 15 minutes, then drain in a sieve.

While the shrimps are soaking, finely slice the garlic. Finely chop the red chilli, dice the pickled *pak choi*, and set aside separately. Cut the garlic sprouts into 3cm (1¼ inch) lengths, then blanch them in boiling water in a wok for 3 minutes. Drain in a sieve, then put them into a bowl of cold water to stop them overcooking. Lightly score the squid bodies diagonally, then cut them into rough chunks, place them in a small bowl or ramekin and mix with the cornflour (cornstarch).

Mix together all the sauce ingredients in a small bowl.

Now build your wok clock: place the garlic at 12 o'clock on the plate, followed by the red chilli, then the squid, blanched garlic sprouts, pickled *pak choi*, dried shrimp and finally the sauce.

Heat the vegetable oil in a wok to a medium heat. When smoking hot, add the garlic and stir-fry until golden brown, then add the red chilli and turn the heat up to high. Once smoking hot again, add the squid and sear, turning everything over once or twice to combine the flavours. Keeping the wok on a high heat, add the garlic sprouts, *pak choi* and dried shrimps, stirring continuously.

After about 30 seconds, stop stirring and allow the wok to heat up even more. Once smoking hot again, pour the sauce into the wok and bring to a vigorous boil. Stir-fry for a further minute, and serve.

SWAPSIES/ALTERNATIVES: ADVICE HERE IS TO KEEP THE GARLIC, CHILLI, SAUCE AND PICKLED PAK CHOI IN THE RECIPE. NO MATTER WHAT OTHER MEAT OR VEG YOU USE THEREAFTER, YOU ARE BOUND TO MAKE ANY STIR-FRY TASTE OUTSTANDING AND UNIQUE WITH THIS SIMPLE COMBINATION OF FLAVOURS. IF YOU ARE GOING FULLY VEGETARIAN, SWAP THE OYSTER SAUCE FOR VEGETARIAN STIR-FRY SAUCE.

韓式泡菜拌扁豆

QUICK PICKLE FLAT GREEN BEANS WITH KIMCHI

200g (7oz) flat green beans
  (swapsies: runner beans)
100g (3½oz/about 1 cup) naturally
  flavoured kimchi
5 sprigs of fresh coriander (cilantro)
1 clove of garlic
1 spring onion (scallion)

THE PICKLING LIQUID
2 tablespoons light soy sauce
5 tablespoons rice vinegar
½ teaspoon salt
1 tablespoon sugar

Slice the green beans at an angle
into roughly 3mm (⅛ inch) thick
pieces. Bring a saucepan of water
to the boil and blanch the beans for
2 minutes. Drain and put them into
a bowl of cold water to cool rapidly.

Roughly chop the kimchi and
coriander (cilantro) and place in a
medium bowl. Finely chop the garlic,
finely slice the spring onion (scallion)
into rings and add both to the bowl.

Put the pickling liquid ingredients
into a small bowl and mix well
together until all the sugar has
melted. Pour over the kimchi mix
and stir well.

Once the beans are cool, drain well,
add to the bowl and mix everything
together. Cover and place in the
fridge until ready to serve. Best
eaten well chilled.

三式蒸蛋

3 STEAMED EGG

This **BEAUTIFUL DISH** is essentially a savoury 'crème caramel' that's all about adding **LAYERS OF TEXTURE** to a bowl of steamed rice, creating a great accompaniment to **ANY HOME-COOKED MEAL.** I have found it even works as a light side to a meaty curry, with some vegetables on the side.

350g (12oz) soft silken tofu
1 preserved century egg (available from Chinese supermarkets)
1 tablespoon light soy sauce
1 teaspoon sugar
½ a spring onion (scallion), green part only

THE EGG MIX
3 eggs
½ teaspoon salt
4 tablespoons water
1 tablespoon vegetable oil

Find a suitable deep-sided plate or steaming dish that will hold all the ingredients in this simple recipe. I use a 20cm (8 inch) Pyrex dish roughly 3–4cm (1¼–1½ inches) deep, which fits everything in perfectly.

First, cut the silken tofu into thin slices roughly 2–3mm (about ⅛ inch) thick and carefully lay them in a stepped circle around the inside of the dish. Crack and peel the century egg, slice it into eighths, then scatter randomly around the dish.

Put the eggs, salt and water into a mixing bowl and mix with a fork, taking care to create as few bubbles as possible, as it will make it difficult to form a smooth surface later. If bubbles do indeed form, run your fork through and carefully remove as many of them as possible. Once you are left with a smooth egg mix, add the vegetable oil and stir in gently. Then carefully pour the egg mix into the dish, fully surrounding the tofu and century egg.

Mix the soy sauce with the sugar, stirring until the sugar has dissolved.

Lastly, finely slice the spring onion greens into rings and place in a bowl of cold water on the side.

Fill a wok with boiling water to come at least one-third to halfway up the sides. Place the tray of egg in a steam basket and cover with a lid.

Put the steam basket directly on top of the wok and steam on a medium to high heat (a rolling boil) for 15 minutes, resisting the temptation to open the lid at all during this time.

Scatter over the finely chopped spring onion to garnish, then pour the sweetened soy sauce over the top and serve.

桂花炒蛋

GUI FA CHOW DAN
(OSMANTHUS FLOWER FRIED EGG)

As with the names of many Chinese dishes, the LITERAL TRANSLATION is less about what is in the dish and more about how it is supposed to look. By cooking the eggs until they start to dry out, they will begin to resemble these TINY LITTLE FLOWERS that the Chinese love to drink as tea. This makes a wonderfully light and savoury breakfast or brunch dish, getting a nice bit of crunchy veg in too!

SERVES 3–4

150g (5oz/about 2½ cups) beansprouts
6 sugar snap peas
10 leaves of little gem lettuce
2 sprigs of fresh coriander (cilantro)
2½ tablespoons vegetable oil
a pinch of sea salt
a pinch of white pepper
3 tablespoons hoisin sauce, for drizzling

THE EGG MIX
3 whole duck eggs
2 additional duck egg yolks
¼ teaspoon salt
½ teaspoon pure sesame oil

THE BLANCHING LIQUID
200ml (7fl oz/about ¾ cup) chicken stock (swapsies: vegetable stock)
1 tablespoon Shaoxing rice wine
¼ teaspoon salt
½ teaspoon sugar

Pick the ends off the beansprouts and wash the sprouts well by soaking in cold water, running your fingers through them a few times, rinsing, then soaking once more in cold water. Finely slice the sugar snap peas into long matchsticks.

In a large wok, bring the blanching liquid ingredients to the boil. Add the beansprouts and blanch for 30 seconds. Immediately scoop them out into a sieve in the sink, then place them in a bowl of cold water to stop them overcooking. Reserve the blanching liquid for later use in the recipe (the excess can be frozen and used as a base for a noodle soup or for general cooking another day).

Beat the egg mix ingredients together in a bowl. Separate the lettuce leaves and have the hoisin sauce ready for drizzling later. Lastly, pick the coriander (cilantro) leaves and place them in a bowl of cold water ready for the garnish.

The skill in cooking this dish comes from lots of stirring with the base of a wok ladle or a flat spatula, as well as using the correct heat on the wok at all times.

Heat 2 tablespoons of oil in a wok to a high heat. Once smoking hot, pour the beaten egg mix into the wok and immediately start to stir, scraping it from the bottom of the wok to avoid any burning or browning of the egg.

After a minute or two, when the egg is about halfway cooked (solidifying, but still relatively wobbly), turn the heat down to medium and continue to stir with the flat part of your spatula to 'scramble' the egg as much as possible. Keep stirring and scraping around the base of the wok until the egg really starts to lose its moisture; it will eventually start to look quite dry and will start to separate out into small, bitty pieces, but it should remain yellow rather than browned (this usually takes 3–4 minutes).

At this point, remove the egg from the wok and tip it into a bowl, then return the wok to the hob on a high heat. Heat ½ tablespoon of vegetable oil to a high heat. Add the sugar snap matchsticks, blanched beansprouts and just 1 tablespoon of the leftover blanching liquid and stir-fry for 30 seconds, then return the scrambled egg back to the wok for one last fold through.

Season with a pinch of sea salt and some white pepper, stir-fry for a further 30 seconds or so, then lightly mix in the coriander leaves.

Serve with the gem lettuce and hoisin sauce on the side, and use the lettuce leaves as cups to hold the scrambled egg and a little drizzle of hoisin.

香菇荷豆粉絲

MUNG BEAN VERMICELLI
WITH SHIITAKE & MANGETOUT

SERVES 4

2 dried shiitake mushrooms
100g (3½oz) dried mung bean
  vermicelli (or glass noodles)
1 clove of garlic
6 mangetout
½ a carrot
1 spring onion (scallion)
50g (1¾oz/about ¾ cup) or approx.
  2 large handfuls of beansprouts
1 tablespoon vegetable oil

THE SAUCE

1 teaspoon chilli bean sauce
1 tablespoon vegetarian stir-fry sauce
  (swapsies: oyster sauce)
½ tablespoon light soy sauce
100ml (3½fl oz/⅓ cup) vegetable
  stock
½ teaspoon pure sesame oil

Soak the dried shiitake mushrooms for at least 1 hour, or overnight for best results.

Soak the mung bean vermicelli in hot water for 3–4 minutes, then drain in a sieve and run cold water from the tap through the noodles to prevent them overcooking.

Finely slice the garlic, and finely matchstick the presoaked and drained mushrooms, mangetout, carrot and spring onion (scallion). Pick the ends off the beansprouts and wash the sprouts well by soaking in cold water, running your fingers through them a few times, rinsing, then soaking once more in cold water.

Mix the sauce ingredients together in a small bowl or ramekin.

Now build your wok clock: place the garlic at 12 o'clock, followed by the carrot, mangetout, mushrooms, beansprouts, soaked vermicelli and then finally your sauce, clockwise around the plate.

Heat 1 tablespoon of vegetable oil in a wok to a high heat. Once smoking hot, add the garlic and stir-fry for 30 seconds, then add the carrot and stir-fry for another 30 seconds. Next, add the mangetout, shiitake mushrooms and the beansprouts and continue stir-frying for 1 minute more, then add the vermicelli, immediately followed by the sauce. Bring the sauce to a vigorous boil, then start to fold the noodles and vegetables through the sauce.

Once all the sauce is evenly coating both the veg and vermicelli, remove from the heat, scatter with the spring onion and serve.

特製辣椒油

HOMEMADE CHILLI OIL

4 cloves of garlic
1 thumb-size piece of ginger
1 large red onion
400ml (14fl oz/1¾ cups) vegetable oil
10 tablespoons chilli flakes

THE SAUCE
1 tablespoon tomato purée
  (tomato paste)
3 tablespoons light soy sauce
1 tablespoon dark soy sauce
1 teaspoon sugar
3 tablespoons water

EQUIPMENT
1 x 250ml (9fl oz) seal-tight jar

Finely chop the garlic, ginger and red onion and set aside. Mix the sauce ingredients together in a small bowl.

Heat 3 tablespoons of the vegetable oil to a medium heat in a saucepan. Once the oil is hot, add the garlic, ginger and red onion and stir, then turn the heat down to low-medium. Continue frying, stirring occasionally, for 10 minutes, until the onions have softened and completely browned. At this point, add the chilli flakes and continue frying on a low heat, stirring intermittently, for 5–6 minutes (turn your extractor fan on high to help with your breathing).

Now turn the heat up to medium-high and add the sauce to the pan. It should start to bubble up quite quickly, with the chilli fumes really hitting your nose at this point. Turn down to a medium heat and continue to stir the mix until it starts to become thicker and 'jammy' in texture. Once thickened, turn the heat down to low and cook until the colour starts to really darken, but not burn. This caramelization should take roughly 20–25 minutes and is what creates the real flavour of the chilli oil. Once you have a thick, dark, reddish brown 'chilli jam', the base of the oil is ready and the pan can be removed from the heat.

Sterilize a 250ml (9fl oz) seal-tight jar by submerging the jar and lid in a large saucepan filled with water and boiling on a low heat for 10 minutes. Once the jar has been sterilized, dry well, then put the chilli jam into the jar and top up with the rest of the vegetable oil. Close the jar and allow to cool completely, then place in the fridge. The chilli oil will taste best after 1 week in the fridge and will keep for 1–2 months.

速製辣椒豉油

QUICK CHILLI SOY SAUCE

My dad used to tell me stories of how he and his siblings would eat when they were growing up, and it used to shock me how different life is for my own siblings and me. At the hardest of times, chilli soy and rice would be the STAPLE DINNER of my father's family. This quick sauce is so TASTY AND VERSATILE, and can be used to flavour almost anything. Try it on the side of noodle soups, simple fried rice, claypot rice, as a dumpling or spring roll dipping sauce, on eggs, or ANYTHING ELSE YOU CAN THINK OF.

1 thumb-size piece of ginger
3 cloves of garlic
2 large red chillies
½ tablespoon sugar
6 tablespoons dark soy sauce
2 tablespoons light soy sauce
1 tablespoon vegetable oil

Bash the piece of ginger with the side of your knife, then roughly chop. Bash the garlic, removing the skins, then roughly chop the garlic and red chillies.

Mix the sugar, dark soy sauce and light soy sauce together in a small bowl or ramekin.

Heat the vegetable oil on a high heat in a wok, then add the ginger, garlic and chilli. Stir-fry for up to 30 seconds, until fragrant and softened, then immediately pour the soy sauce and sugar mix into the wok. Bring to the boil, then turn off the heat straight away. Pour the chilli soy into a ramekin or dipping sauce bowl, ready to serve with whatever else you are making.

Best to keep in the fridge once cool, and to consume within 2–3 days of making.

鮮製辣椒醬

FRESH CHILLI SAUCE

½ a thumb-size piece of ginger
4 cloves of garlic
10 large red chillies

THE HOT LIQUID
3 tablespoons rice vinegar
3 tablespoons hot vegetable stock
1 teaspoon salt
½ teaspoon sugar
1 teaspoon pure sesame oil

Roughly chop the ginger, garlic and chillies and place in a food processor. Put all the hot liquid ingredients into a small saucepan and bring to the boil. Once the sugar has melted, switch the hob off and pour the hot liquid into a food processor. Pulse until a paste-like consistency has formed.

Set aside, cover and chill, ready to use as you wish. Once cooled, keep in the fridge and consume within 2 or 3 days of making.

Travelling through Hong Kong you are likely to bypass the many dessert houses and bakeries that the city has to offer, often without even noticing them. I find it fascinating that such a huge city has so many establishments whose menus are 90 per cent sweet, yet still has such a notoriously bad reputation for desserts.

The Chinese are certainly not famous for their desserts, and I would happily agree that the French can take the reins when it comes to the fine art of pâtisserie. However, over the years and through both research and my own leanings towards my Chinese heritage, I've started to really understand where this lack of fame may come from. To a Chinese person, a dessert is not just something that we eat at the end of the meal. A dessert is something that can be eaten at any time of the day, much like savoury dishes in the Chinese tradition. Food is simply there for enjoyment and cannot (or should not) be held to such strict regulations and conformities as to what time of day it is to be eaten!

The thing about eating roadside in a busy city like Hong Kong is that with the constant heaving crowds of people, it often becomes difficult to

see café fronts and signs, making it that much harder to distinguish your man-and-a-pan *dai pai dongs* and specialist restaurants from one another – they all look the same when you can see only one small corner of them!

In response to this needle-in-a-haystack situation, some of the biggest chains of dessert houses have created inviting, open-fronted, visibly and vibrantly colourful façades to their cafés, serving fresh mango and pomelo juice, squeezed en masse. And with the often hot and humid weather of Hong Kong, these sprawling ice-cold fruit juice, sago or tapioca and milk tea cafés are a welcome pit-stop.

A true Hong Kong eating tour wouldn't be complete without a visit to one of the city's bakeries, specializing in gloriously fluffy, sweet baked buns and cakes. This type of dessert is so popular and delicious, in fact, that my grandfather made his living as a baker, running one of the oldest standing bakeries in the London and Manchester Chinatowns. Perhaps I am biased because of this lineage, but one of my guiltiest pleasures and comforts, which I turn to when missing Hong Kong, is a steamed cake or crumbly 'pineapple' bun. There is just no substitute.

洗手間設於商場內
PLEASE USE THE TOILET INSIDE THE SHOPPING MALL

小心地滑

甜品及飲料
DESSERTS & DRINKS

港式奶茶

HONG KONG MILK TEA

If such a thing as a 'NATIONAL DRINK' exists, Hong Kong milk tea would be the most obvious contender for this title. Every *cha chaan teng*, streetside café and restaurant will have its own milk tea, served either hot or ice-cold and made with evaporated milk or condensed milk as opposed to fresh milk. As the photographer for this book, Kris, remarked, drinking it feels like a HUG IN A MUG. It's also another classic example of how the post-war food culture that developed in Hong Kong is still very much alive.

SERVES 2–3

2 tablespoons Pu'er or Bo Lei tea leaves (swapsies: 3 Yorkshire tea bags or any strong black tea)
500ml (18fl oz/2 cups) boiling water
50–100g (2–3½oz/¼–½ cup) condensed milk (depending on your desired level of sweetness)

Put the tea leaves or tea bags into the boiling water and boil for 5 minutes, to get the tea nice and strong. Add the condensed milk and stir well with a whisk to create a little froth. Pour from a height to add more froth, and serve. You can serve this as is, or let it cool down and pour it over ice for a refreshing treat.

杏仁金寶曲奇

ALMOND CRUMBLE COOKIES

½ the crumble topping from the Pineapple Bun recipe on page 159, or any leftover crumble topping
50g (1¾oz) flaked almonds

Preheat the oven to 200°C/180°C fan (400°F).

Roll the crumble topping into a long cylinder roughly 4cm (1½ inches) in diameter. Slice the cylinder into 1cm (½ inch) rounds. Place the rounds on a baking tray lined with greaseproof paper, leaving at least 1cm (½ inch) between the cookies. Lightly press a scattering of flaked almonds into the centre of each one.

Bake on the middle shelf of the oven for 12 minutes, until the cookies are lightly browned around the edges. Remove from the oven and leave to cool for 5 minutes on the tray before placing on a cooling rack.

Once the cookies are at room temperature, put into an airtight container to keep them crunchy. They will keep for 3–4 days. Enjoy with a cup of Hong Kong milk tea!

花生醬奶油多

PEANUT BUTTER FRENCH TOAST
WITH CONDENSED MILK

What a strange dessert – so MOREISHLY ADDICTIVE you will not be able to resist tucking in for another bite. In Hong Kong, this dish is more of a MIDDAY SNACK than a dessert, so feel free to follow suit. Try it as a midnight snack, as a dessert or even for a weekend breakfast. ANY-TIME-OF-DAY EATING, Hong Kong style.

MAKES 8

16 slices of white bread
3 eggs
16 tablespoons smooth
　peanut butter
vegetable oil, for frying
300g (10½oz/1½ cups)
　condensed milk

Spread one slice of bread with condensed milk, and a second with 2 tablespoons of peanut butter, adding a bit extra in the very centre of the slice. Stick the 2 slices together, with the fillings in the centre of the sandwich. Repeat this process until all your sandwiches have been made.

Now, in a bowl the width of the bread, whisk together your eggs. Submerge the sandwich completely in the eggs, then allow the extra egg to drip off. Now you can either pan-fry the French toast in hot oil over a medium high heat until golden brown all over, or you can deep-fry the bread as follows:

Half-fill a large pot, wok or deep-fryer with vegetable oil and heat to 180°C (350°F), or use a wooden skewer or wooden chopstick to test by placing the tip in the oil: if the wood starts to fizz after a second or so, the oil is hot enough.

Using a slotted spoon or a Chinese frying skimmer, carefully lay the eggy bread sandwiches in the oil. Once one side is golden brown, turn over and fry the other side. Once golden brown all over, remove from the oil and place on a couple of pieces of kitchen paper to drain off any excess oil. Repeat until you have fried all your sandwiches.

Slice the sandwiches in half diagonally to serve, then cover with a generous drizzle of condensed milk.

健舅父菠蘿包

UNCLE KEN'S BO LO BAO – BAKED PINEAPPLE BUNS

My UNCLE KEN is the baker of our family, having inherited the skill and natural baker's touch from my grandfather. One challenge that comes with inheriting family recipes however, is that in my grandfather's day, nothing was ever really measured – so every time my uncle kindly passes down a recipe to me, the measurements seem to come in a variety of different forms. This particular recipe, from Uncle Ken, read, 'Just THROW TOGETHER a sack-full of flour, three-quarters of a Chinese rice bowl of sugar, a bit of margarine or butter, and enough water to make the dough perfect.' After a few tries and my trusty scales, I have to say this recipe really does make the same kind of pineapple buns (named after the shape of the crumble topping, resembling the outside of a pineapple, rather than having pineapple in the recipe itself) you'd find in any good HONG KONG BAKERY. Thanks, Uncle Ken, I'm proud to be your baking disciple.

TIP: THERE IS PURPOSELY MORE CRUMBLE TOPPING IN THIS RECIPE THAN IS NEEDED, IN CASE YOU NEED MORE BECAUSE OF BREAKAGES OR SLIGHT ACCIDENTS. SEE PAGE 156 FOR WHAT TO DO WITH THE EXTRA BISCUIT-LIKE CRUMBLE ONCE THE BUNS HAVE BEEN MADE. TWO TREATS HATCHED FROM ONE RECIPE IS MY KIND OF COOKING!

MAKES 8–10

THE BREAD DOUGH

400g (14oz/3 cups) strong bread flour
70g (2½oz/about ⅓ cup) caster sugar (superfine sugar)
½ teaspoon salt
½ teaspoon organic bread/dough improver (optional, but you can find this easily online)
7g (just under ¼oz or 1 sachet) fast-action dried yeast
25g (1oz) margarine
200ml (7fl oz/¾ cup) warm water (about 30–35°C/85–95°F)
1 tablespoon vegetable oil

THE CRUMBLE TOPPING

200g (7oz/just under 1 cup) butter
200g (7oz/1 cup) caster sugar (superfine sugar)
1 egg, plus extra beaten egg for the eggwash
1 teaspoon vanilla extract
1 small dab of yellow food colouring (optional)
200g (7oz/1½ cups) plain flour (all-purpose flour)
200g (7oz/1½ cups) self-raising flour (self-rising flour)

Put the dry bread dough ingredients into an electric mixer fitted with a dough hook, add the margarine, and start to mix at a low speed.

Gradually pour in the warm water, until all the flour has come off the edge of the mixer. Turn the speed up to high and knead for 3–4 minutes, until the dough becomes a little 'stringy' in texture – tacky and slightly moist. Remove from the mixer and knead by hand for a minute or so, then roll into one large ball and put back into the mixing bowl. Rub 1 tablespoon of vegetable oil all over the dough, then cover the bowl with a clean damp tea towel.

Place in a warm, humid environment and allow to rise for 1–1½ hours (see tip on page 160).

Once the dough has doubled in size, knock it back by punching into it a few times and shaping it into a rough ball once more, then allow to prove for a further 30 minutes, in the same humid and warm environment.

Now make the crumble topping. Whisk the butter and sugar together until light and fluffy. Add the egg and whisk in well, either by hand or on a medium speed in a dough mixer with the k-hook attachment. Once the egg has been well combined with the butter and sugar, add the vanilla extract and the yellow food colouring, if using, then sift both the flours into the bowl and slowly combine all the ingredients together, either with your hands, or, if using the dough mixer, on speed 1. (The yellow food colouring will help to enhance the changes in colour across the crumble topping, giving you that classic Hong Kong bakery 'pineapple' effect.)

Once well mixed, the crumble topping should resemble a cookie dough. Remove from the bowl and roll out on a floured surface to about 3–4mm (⅛ inch) thick. Use an 8–9cm (3¼ inch) round cookie cutter to cut the crumble topping into circles the correct size to cover the buns. Use the back of a butter knife to gently make a criss-cross pattern on each crumble topping surface, but make sure not to cut through completely.

By the time you've finished your topping, the dough should have doubled in size once more. Shape it into 8–10 buns, as follows: roll the dough into a large cylinder, then cut into pieces roughly 6–7cm

(2½ inches) wide. Roll each piece into a smooth ball and place on a baking tray lined with greaseproof paper. Once all the bun shapes have been made, cover once more with the damp tea towel and place in the same humid, warm place for a final 15–20 minutes to prove one last time.

Preheat the oven to 200°C/180°C fan (400°F). Brush the top of each bun with beaten egg, then carefully place a circle of crumble over each of the buns. Add another coat of eggwash over the crumble filling and bake in the oven for 15–20 minutes, until the top of the crumble is golden brown and crispy. The buns should rise by at least 50% more while baking.

TIP: ONE WAY TO HELP YOUR DOUGH RISE IS TO PREHEAT YOUR OVEN TO ABOUT 40°C (100°F) FOR 10–15 MINUTES WHILE THE DOUGH IS BEING KNEADED, WITH A SMALL, METAL BOWL OF BOILING HOT WATER PLACED IN THE BOTTOM OF THE OVEN. TURN THE OVEN OFF AND IMMEDIATELY PUT THE DOUGH INTO THE OVEN TO RISE, PLACING THE BOWL ON THE MIDDLE SHELF.

楊枝金露

MANGO & POMELO SAGO

SERVES 6–8

½ a pomelo fruit
1 large ripe mango
100ml (3½fl oz/⅓ cup) coconut milk

THE MANGO SORBET
250g (9oz) fresh ripe mango
  pieces, puréed
100ml (3½fl oz/⅓ cup) water
100ml (3½fl oz/⅓ cup) lime juice
100g (3½oz/about ½ cup) caster
  sugar (superfine sugar)

THE SAGO SYRUP
50g (1¾oz) rock sugar
600ml (20fl oz/2½ cups) cold water
150g (5oz/1 cup) dried tapioca pearls
  (sago)

THE MANGO PULP
250ml (9fl oz/1 cup) mango juice
250ml (9fl oz) cold mango purée, or
  fresh ripe mango

First make the mango sorbet by blending all the sorbet ingredients together in a blender. Place in a small Tupperware, covered with a lid, and put into the freezer overnight.

Put the sago syrup ingredients into a saucepan and bring to the boil, then lower the heat to a simmer, stirring continuously for 25–30 minutes to ensure that the tapioca cooks evenly. Once the tapioca looks translucent, cover with a lid and leave to cool. It will end up with the consistency of slightly watery jelly.

Peel the pomelo, then extract the flesh from each segment, discarding the pith. Peel the mango and slice into 1cm (½ inch) cubes.

Add 2–3 tablespoons of sago syrup to each bowl. Then, in a blender, blend the mango pulp ingredients together and pour into individual serving bowls. To assemble the dessert, pour a swirl or two of coconut milk over the top of the mango pulp, scatter a generous portion of the pomelo and mango bits over the top, and finish with a scoop of mango sorbet.

蛋撻

DAN TAT – CHEAT'S EGG TARTS

In **PROFESSIONAL BAKERIES**, the cake ovens tend to be bottom-heating, which allows the base of the pastry to crisp up while controlling any caramelization on the top of the tarts. Therefore, baking egg tarts at home isn't going to yield the same results when it comes to their perfect butter-yellow uniform crust. However, by embracing a **RUSTIC 'I MADE THESE AT HOME' LOOK** to your egg tarts, you will be rewarded by the contrast of textures between the **MELT-IN-THE-MOUTH** creamy filling and the flaky, buttery puff pastry.

MAKES 20 TARTS

2 sheets of ready-rolled puff pastry
a little plain flour (all-purpose flour),
  for dusting

THE SYRUP
180g (6oz/just under 1 cup) caster
  sugar (superfine sugar)
300ml (10fl oz/1¼ cups) water
2 pandan leaves (optional)

THE EGG MIXTURE
4 eggs, beaten
225ml (8fl oz/1 cup) syrup
  (see above)
60ml (2fl oz/¼ cup) water

EQUIPMENT
20 muffin tins, fairy cake tins or
  egg tart cases

Preheat the oven to its highest temperature.

In a small saucepan, mix the syrup ingredients together and bring to the boil. Over a medium heat, reduce the syrup by about half (you need to end up with 225ml/8fl oz/1 cup), then remove from the heat and leave to cool.

In a mixing bowl, combine the eggs and cooled syrup and pass through a sieve twice, to remove the stringy parts of the eggs. To avoid excess caramelization and potential burning when cooking, carefully remove any bubbles from the egg mix by skimming the bubbles off the top with a fork, then wiping around the sides of the bowl with kitchen paper to remove any smaller bubbles at the edge.

Dust your work surface with plain (all-purpose) flour to prevent the pastry sticking, then, using a 7cm (2¾ inch) round cookie cutter, cut the ready-rolled puff pastry into circles. Line 20 muffin tins, fairy cake tins or egg tart cases, if available, with the pastry and press it firmly into place, making sure the pastry is flush against the sides to prevent bubbling during baking.

Just before putting the tarts into the oven, bring the heat down to 230°C/210°C fan (450°F). Place the tart cases on a baking tray and pour some of the filling into each tart, taking care not to fill them any more than two-thirds of the way up.

Place the tarts on the middle shelf of the oven, making sure there is another spare wire shelf above, and bake for 8 minutes.

After 8 minutes, turn the oven down to 210°C/190°C fan (410°F) and slide a cool baking tray on to the shelf just above the egg tarts, to stop the filling browning too much. Bake for a further 8–10 minutes, until the filling starts to 'dome'. Once this happens, the tarts should be cooked through. Remove from the oven and allow to cool slightly before serving.

班丹瑞士卷

BRIGHT GREEN PANDAN SWISS ROLL

THE PANDAN SWISS ROLL
120g (4¼oz/just under 1 cup) plain
flour (all-purpose flour)
¼ teaspoon baking powder
160g (5¾oz/¾ cup) caster sugar
(superfine sugar)
125ml (4fl oz/½ cup) boiling water
9 whole eggs, at room temperature
¾ teaspoon pandan concentrate
(not essence)
60ml (2fl oz/¼ cup) vegetable oil

THE CHANTILLY CREAM
400g (14oz/2 cups) whipping cream
or double cream (heavy cream)
200g (7oz/1½ cups) icing sugar
(confectioners' sugar)
1½ teaspoon vanilla extract

TO ASSEMBLE
1 jar of raspberry jam

Preheat the oven to 220°C/200°C
fan (425°F). Sift the flour and baking
powder into a mixing bowl. In a
separate mixing bowl or an electric
dough mixer, whisk the caster sugar
(superfine sugar) and boiling water
together to make a syrup (medium
speed in a mixer, or whisk by hand)
for 3–4 minutes.

Once the sugar has dissolved, add
the eggs, then whisk on high speed
(or vigorously by hand) for 3–4
minutes. The mixture will become
creamy and fluffy and should
expand to roughly three times its
volume, as you beat air into the mix.
Add the pandan concentrate and
whisk for 30 seconds, until the mix
has a uniform, bright green colour.

Now, across the top of the mix,
evenly sift the flour and baking
powder. Gently fold the flour into
the egg mix by hand, until it is all
well incorporated and no lumps
remain, taking care to fold from
bottom to top carefully, retaining
as much air in the mix as possible.

Pour the vegetable oil all the way
around the edge of the mixing bowl,
then quickly fold the oil into the mix.
This is a critical part of the sponge-
making – if it takes too long, you
will lose a certain amount of volume
and the cake may sink in the oven.

Rub butter around a 60cm (24 inch)
baking tray, then line with good-
quality baking paper or silicone
paper. Give the cake mix one last
fold, to scrape any excess flour from
the bottom, then pour the mix on
to the lined baking tray.

Place the baking tray on the middle
shelf of the oven, with a spare wire
shelf underneath, for 12 minutes
(the top will start to brown by this
point). Now place a room temperature
oven tray underneath the cake tray
in the oven, guarding the bottom
of the cake from too much heat.
Turn the oven down to 180°C/160°C
fan (350°F) and bake for a further
14 minutes.

Once cooked, remove the cake
from the oven, checking that it
is cooked through by poking a
toothpick into the centre of the
cake – if it comes out completely
clean, the cake is ready. Take the

cake off the baking tray and place
immediately on a cooling rack for
3 minutes. Then place a sheet of
baking paper or silicone paper over
the top of the cake. Holding a cool
baking tray on top, carefully flip the
cake upside down on to the cool
tray and place on a work surface.

Remove the top layer of paper.
Cut the sides of the cake off, so as
to expose the bright green colour,
then immediately roll the cake into
a tight Swiss roll shape (this helps
to keep the cake flexible for rolling
up again later). Roll it tight all the
way up, like a Swiss roll, carefully
removing the bottom sheet of paper
as you go. Once fully rolled, allow
to cool completely.

Whisk the Chantilly cream ingredients
together until the cream has
thickened and then place in the
fridge to cool for 30 minutes. Unroll
the cooled sponge and spread it
with a roughly 2mm (1/16 inch) thick
layer of raspberry jam. On top of the
jam, spread about 3–4mm (1/8 inch)
of Chantilly cream. Now roll the cake
back up once more (like a large sushi
roll) to form a Swiss roll. Traditionally
in Hong Kong bakeries, this is
then cut into 3–4cm (1¼–1½ inch)
pieces, to be served on individual
cake plates for a stunning and
colourful treat.

TIP: IF MAKING THE SWISS ROLL WELL IN
ADVANCE AND DO NOT WANT TO RUN THE
RISK OF YOUR WHIPPED CREAM MELTING,
WHILE WAITING FOR GUESTS, TRY USING
DREAM WHIP OR AN EQUIVALENT 'WHIPPED'
CREAM ALTERNATIVE INSTEAD.

馬拉糕

STEAMED CHINESE SPONGE

340g (12oz/2½ cups) self-raising
  flour (self-rising flour)
340g (12oz/2 cups) brown sugar
5 medium eggs
200ml (7fl oz/¾ cup) vegetable oil
28g (1oz) baking powder
200ml (7fl oz/¾ cup) evaporated milk
2 teaspoons custard powder
¼ teaspoon bicarbonate of soda
  (baking soda)
½ teaspoon vanilla extract

Put all the ingredients into the bowl of an electric mixer fitted with a whisk attachment and fold together on a low speed (no higher than speed 2). Once all the ingredients are well combined, change the mixer speed to high for 2–3 minutes. The sponge mix should now resemble a thick, airy batter. Leave to rest for 10 minutes.

Meanwhile, set a steamer up. Ideally, use a large stockpot as the base to create the steam, so that you do not need to keep topping up the water. Place a steam stand or metal bowl in the base of the pot, then fill the stockpot one-third of the way up with water and bring to the boil.

Grease the sides and base of a high-sided 18–20cm (7–8 inch) cake tin (mine is roughly 18cm/7 inches in diameter x 10cm/4 inches tall) with

a little butter or oil. Beat the batter once more to create a few larger air bubbles, then pour it into the greased cake tin. Place carefully in the steamer on top of the steam stand, then cover with a lid wrapped in a clean tea towel, or with a bamboo steamer lid that fits on top of the stockpot, to stop any condensation dripping on to the cake.

Steam the cake for 50 minutes, resisting the urge to lift the lid at all unless you have to top up the hot water (in which case, do so quickly so as not to lose too much steam). After 50 minutes, lift the lid and check that the cake is cooked all the way through by piercing the middle with a bamboo skewer. If the skewer comes out clean, without any trace of raw cake mix, it is ready. If not, put the lid back on and steam for a further 10 minutes.

燉奶

STEAMED MILK PUDDINGS

SERVES 4

25ml (1 fl oz) squeezed ginger juice
 (from roughly 2–3 thumb-size
 pieces of ginger, see method)
550ml (19fl oz/2¼ cups) milk
75g (2¾oz/about ⅓ cup) caster
 sugar (superfine sugar)
4 egg whites

EQUIPMENT
4 small Chinese rice bowls

To make the ginger juice, finely chop the ginger, then place in a clean tea towel and squeeze tightly over a small bowl, twisting the tea towel round and round to squeeze out the juice.

In a saucepan, heat the milk and sugar together on a medium heat, stirring occasionally, until the sugar has dissolved, taking care not to let it boil. Once the milk is scalding hot but not boiling, remove from the heat.

Beat the egg whites in a bowl with a fork until foamy. Pour the ginger juice into the milk mix, then gradually add the milk mix to the egg whites, mixing well until all is combined. Pour the mix through a sieve twice, to get rid of any stringy bits of egg white and excess foam. Remove any remaining foam by dabbing with a folded piece of kitchen paper and pressing against the edge of the bowl. Once all the bubbles and foam have been removed, pour carefully into small Chinese rice bowls.

Now set up a steamer. Ideally, use a large stockpot as the base to create the steam, so that you don't need to keep topping up the water. Place a steam stand in the pot, then fill the stockpot one-third of the way up with water. Bring to the boil, then turn the heat down low so as not to steam the puddings too quickly.

Wrap the lid in a clean tea towel to avoid dripping water from the steam on to the puddings. Carefully place the bowls in the steam tray, cover with the lid and steam for 20–25 minutes on a low heat. Be sure to lift the lid off the steamer every 5 minutes – this allows the excess steam out and helps the pudding to set without too much water building up on top. A skin should form on the top of the milk pudding once set. If eating cold, allow to cool fully and another layer of skin will form on the top of the pudding.

迷你桂香沙翁

CINNAMON SUGAR MINI BAO DOUGHNUTS

1 portion of *bao* dough (see page 62)
vegetable oil, for frying

TO SERVE
10g (¼oz) ground cinnamon
90g (3¼oz/about ⅓ cup) caster
 sugar (superfine sugar)
condensed milk

Make 1 portion of *bao* dough
and allow to prove for 1½ hours.

Roll the proved *bao* dough into
a long cylinder, roughly 3–4cm
(1¼–1½ inches) in diameter, then
cut into 3–4cm (1¼–1½ inch) thick
pieces. Roll each piece of dough
in your hands to form a smooth ball.
Cover the balls with a damp cloth
and set aside to rest for a further
15–20 minutes.

Meanwhile, set a steamer up. Place
bao on squares of greaseproof
paper and then steam for 8 minutes
in a covered steam basket, inside
a wok half-filled with boiling water,
without opening the lid, until
cooked through and risen well.

At this stage you can either pan-fry
your dough balls over a medium-
high heat until golden brown, or
deep-fry them for 2–3 minutes
in either a wok or a deep-fat fryer.
To deep-fry them, half-fill a large

pot, wok or deep-fryer with
vegetable oil and heat to 180°C
(350°F), or use a wooden skewer
or wooden chopstick to test by
placing the tip in the oil: if the wood
starts to fizz after a second or so,
the oil is hot enough.

Once the oil is hot enough, carefully
lay the steamed *baos*, round side
down, in the oil and fry for 1 minute
or so until golden brown. Turn once
and fry for a further 30 seconds
to a minute to crisp up the bottom.
Gently roll them around in the oil
so they cook evenly.

Once cooked using your method
of choice, roll them in a mix of
cinnamon and caster sugar
(superfine sugar) and serve
alongside a bowl of condensed
milk, for dipping.

INDEX

JEREMY'S ACKNOWLEDGEMENTS

My Chinese cooking is far better than my embarrassing attempt to speak Chinese. It's not even worth me pretending. However, something that I have always found fascinating about Chinese prose are the four to five word phrases or idioms that seem to make up the most part of the Chinese spoken language, even today. In general, they are short phrases with deep meaning. One such phrase that my dad always talked about was this one: 富不过三代, which roughly translates as 'wealth does not pass three generations'.

If you are like me (as Adrienne describes, a big kid, who doesn't believe in words of wisdom), then these wise words and idioms are there to be discussed and debated. I like to think that food is the simplest, and perhaps the most important wealth in life and is an easy contender to whoever made up this phrase. Knowledge in food can be passed down from one generation to another quite simply, and the joy of food and sharing, which is the epitome of the Chinese dinner table, can inspire all generations to want to learn more and nurture such wealth.

Family and friends are at the heart of every recipe and meal that I cook and create, and this book clearly takes inspiration from my nearest and dearest. Market style cheung fun, fried stuffed tofu and influence from visits to dim sum houses at 6am after a swim with the oldies off the coast of Ma On Shan are by no means my own creations. Rather, they are memories shared with my sisters Wendy and Jen from our years in and out of Hong Kong spending quality time with our parents. Mum practically made the mango and pomelo sago that has been photographed in the book to save me time on the 40 odd recipes we had to shoot. After all, it is the type of recipe that mums like to make by the masses so it kept us all going during the shoot. Her knowledge of Hong Kong is second to none, and she was crucial in the planning and translation stages – thanks a million for being the best mum. Also, huge thanks to Dee, my wife, for allowing me to gallivant around Hong Kong during some of the toughest parts of pregnancy and then letting us turn our home into a photo studio for the rest of the shots and generally being an inspiration to me and Theo throughout this whole time.

Team Quadrille (Sarah Lavelle, Helen Lewis, Nikki Ellis, Amy Christian, Annie Lee, Jim Smith) for believing in me once again and putting the time and effort into making this book as bright and colourful as Hong Kong deserves it to be. Kris Kirkham and Hannah Hughes for throwing themselves in the deep end on the photography front both in Hong Kong and of course joining the *Chinese Unchopped* dream-team with Camilla Baynham and Iris Bromet food and prop stylist extraordinaires. Once again, thanks Freya Deabill for such playful illustrations. Heather Byres for helping with all the chopping and cooking, who at the time was our School of Wok intern, and whilst on shoot, found herself a full-time job with us, which we all quite rightly cheered for.

And of course, team #PangTours, the avid eaters: Nev, Max, Mark, John and Tor. And last but not least, Adrienne Katz Kennedy, who over the last five years has become almost as 'British Born Chinese' as I am, and has taken to the role as contributing author like noodles to a wok, which of course, I never doubted she would. Long may our writing together continue.

ADRIENNE'S ACKNOWLEDGEMENTS

To the people of Hong Kong; Jeremy's generous family, Kenny and Bill, the mighty #PangTours entourage: John, Tor, Mark, Nev, Max and Kris, the locals we slurped soup with, who (mostly) tolerated our cameras and questions, the dim sum ladies I watched so intensely at Tai Po market, the dai pai dong chefs whose space I invaded unintentionally to look inside their woks, street artist Grand, whose work now hangs in many homes in London. THANK YOU for sharing a bit of your life and your lunch with me; it has been an experience of a lifetime. Truly HLC.

To Jeremy, my writing partner, 'boss' and friend, for opening up my eyes to a culture I only knew the half of, and then trusting me to write accurately, personally and passionately about it; this has been a pleasure and a privilege. Where to next (and can we please walk a bit slower next time)?

To my grandma, who taught me that food and words were the most powerful and pleasurable tools I had access to, how I wish you were here so I could describe everything I ate to you.

To my mama, who flew across the world to help out so I could fly off on adventure, thank you for your constant support. To my dad, who has stayed the course through many weird performances and choices, both metaphorically and literally speaking, thank you for trusting me to land on my feet.

To Nell and Isla, who if they had it their way would eat everything on either a stick or by chopsticks, I can't wait to show you this part of the world, and all the rest of it.

To my husband Nick who has painstakingly read every word I have written in the last ten years; thank you for being my editor and my everything.

First published in 2017 by Quadrille,
an imprint of Hardie Grant Publishing
Quadrille, 52–54 Southwark Street,
London SE1 1UN
quadrille.co.uk

Text © 2017 Jeremy Pang & Adrienne Katz Kennedy
Photography © Kris Kirkham
Design and layout © 2017 Quadrille Publishing
With thanks to Mark Campbell

Cataloguing in Publication Data: a catalogue record
for this book is available from the British Library.

Reprinted in 2018 (twice)
10 9 8 7 6 5 4 3

ISBN: 978-1-84949-992-7

Printed in China

Publishing Director: Sarah Lavelle
Creative Director: Helen Lewis
Photographic Art Direction: Nicola Ellis
Design: Helen Lewis, Jim Smith
Illustrations: Freya Deabill
Project Editor: Amy Christian
Copy Editor: Annie Lee
Photographer: Kris Kirkham
Food stylist: Camilla Baynham
Prop stylist: Iris Bromet
Production: Vincent Smith and Nikolaus Ginelli

#PANGTOURS
OUR REFERENCE GUIDE TO HONG KONG EATING

THE BEAUTY OF THE DAILY SHOP AND MARKET CULTURE

Hong Kong residents are spoiled for choice when it comes to fresh markets, wet markets, butchers, specialist shops and cafés – from tiny eateries that serve only stuffed or braised tofu dishes, to market stalls that sell only pantry ingredients and pickled vegetables, to greengrocers, fishmongers, butchers and the like. Food shopping is much less about stockpiling ingredients under the fluorescent lights of the big box supermarkets, or the hurried point-and-click online grocery delivery services we big-city Westerners have become so accustomed to. Rather, residents do their shopping in noisy daily markets, each stand serving or supplying a short list of excellent, well-chosen ingredients, products or dishes. No matter what the stall specializes in, whether it is vegetables, meats or pantry ingredients, each place of business concentrates on homing in on only its very best, rather than the split focus of trying to have it all.

Consequently, by shopping in this manner, despite the few extra minutes of time or effort involved each day, Hong Kongers create little waste in their homes. Meals are planned, shopped for, cooked and eaten with little left behind; partially because of the limited space to store 'extras' and partially because this method does not forgive those whose eyes are bigger than their woks. Shop, cook, eat, repeat, is the mantra of daily Hong Kong life, and as a result fresh, seasonal ingredients are naturally consumed, without the need to rely on the influence of marketing a 'lifestyle' to keep it going. There is little other choice. In fact, there are even stalls, like those seen at Tai Po market, which offer fresh fruit and veg that are bruised and therefore perhaps less desirable, or that will need to be used that day before they are too ripe, wilted or old, at a reduced rate. The value of living a wasteless and resourceful life is ever present, from the types of dishes that make up the cuisine, to the strong market culture.

RESTAURANT DÉCOR: NOTHING HIDDEN, NOTHING REMOVED

Hong Kong restaurant décor, as we discovered, is rough and ready. Cheap plastic tables and chairs, unmemorable and often cracked tiles, fluorescent lights, melamine bowls, thick plastic chopsticks and the thinnest and smallest paper napkins known to man. Let's just say that unlike what we have come to know in the UK, you can't spot a Michelin-starred restaurant in Hong Kong by its bathrooms. It is not because of lack of care, but rather that there is little value placed on the interior and much more on the quality of the ingredients and dishes that come out of it.

From the apparent prep work and raw materials displayed upon a front window table until they are put to use, to the animals: cooked with heads and feet still intact and sometimes even on display, nothing is hidden from the public in Hong Kong street food/diner culture. Customers see the work put into the food, the association with the once live animal, and the breakdown of costs. No gimmick, no particular mystery behind the preparation, no detachment from the process. It feels straightforward to the point of trustworthy.

Stepping into the kitchen of most of these eateries (provided they were big enough for us to fit!), we discovered everything to be freshly made, often hand-selected from the market that morning, then picked apart, butchered, cleaned and prepped by a small handful of worker bees in Wellington boots and aprons, cooking on industrial burners with flames that would singe your eyebrows with just one wrong flick of the wok, before being served quickly and efficiently. Many local restaurants are run by families, with no one too young or aged to contribute. This only reiterates the transparency and authenticity of these small cafés and diners – even Grandpa is not hidden away. In some cases, such as our experience at a *cha chaan teng* from 1954, tucked away in an unassuming corner of a busy side street, the original owner still at the till, chatting to customers as they paid and of course making sure every penny went to the right place.

THE CHINESE MEAL EXPERIENCE

Food in Hong Kong is delivered and consumed at a rapid-fire pace. Upon first glance it could easily be attributed to the cosmopolitan cityscape, but it is far less about the need to keep up with a moving busy city and more about how the Chinese eat in general.

The idea of 'courses' is a Western concept. Unless at a wedding banquet, courses, during a traditional Chinese meal, are eaten all at once, served family-style on one heaving, typically round, table filled with an array of flavours, textures and colours. Everyone takes from the same 10 (or more!) dishes, eating each mouthful over a bowl of steamed white rice, which then soaks up any drips of sauce and mishaps with the chopsticks. Each bite consumed is different, with chopsticks flying and weaving over and under one another to get to the food.

A sense of closeness is created between those sitting around the table, merely from the amount of shared space and interaction it takes to get the food from the table into mouths. Relationships are formed through this way of shared, intimate family-style eating. It is something Western restaurant culture cannot quite match. Unless sitting round someone's dinner table in their own home, no Western-style restaurant experience I've ever had has quite reached this level of immediate familial and overlapping co-existence like the meals I had in Hong Kong. Even from my very first meal with Jeremy and a few others I barely knew, if at all, the instant shared experience of passing dishes, leaning over each other with our long plastic chopsticks in an attempt to nab morsels from the various serving platters, and the doling out of rice helped to develop an instant closeness and sense of community that would carry on throughout the trip. The way in which meals were consumed at a wide variety of eateries, from those with tablecloths, to those without usable bathrooms, cannot help but flag up two undeniable and most valued aspects in Chinese culture: food and family. One seems impossible without the other.

HONG KONG STREET FOOD & NIGHT CULTURE

Street food is alive and well in Hong Kong; one can greedily feast for hours without breaking the bank. For example: one warm, neon sign-lit evening on the streets of Mong Kok, I found myself guilty of having consumed essentially a banquet feast, eaten in snack-sized increments every 10 minutes or so, never realizing just how much we had consumed over a few short hours. Jeremy grew up with this style of eating, enjoying frequent trips to Hong Kong, where his parents were both from. In true #Pangtours style, he made it his mission to train up his Hong Kong entourage into

prolonged feasters, powered by equal parts enjoyment and curiosity. It came as no surprise that the streets of Hong Kong easily sustained and encouraged this continuous ability to 'eat something' with a wide array of amazing delights.

On this one particular night as we wandered the night markets, we began the feast with a little snack of Shanghai-style grilled chive dumplings, then curried fish balls, fishcake-stuffed green peppers and aubergines, ending with an eggette (Hong Kong style waffle), pineapple buns and steamed custard buns for dessert. And that was before two additional courses and a beer at a *dai pai dong* later that evening!

During this seemingly endless feast I found myself constantly surrounded by all walks of life, from those carried in the arms of their parents to those who walked with the aid of a stick. Street culture is for the young and old, wealthy and poor, local and tourist.

Throughout the trip we sat around cheap plastic tables, feasting in the midst of alleys and bustling markets with businessmen wearing designer suits, and equally among those with little more than the clothes on their back. The eateries in which we were dining always seemed conscious of what their customers could afford, and priced accordingly – both feeding and caring for the local community. Perhaps it's a biased rose-tinted view, but it felt like eateries were more concerned with being a part of the local landscape, rather than just the size of their profit.

Street food culture in Hong Kong meant babies were out long after dark, mixed in with throngs of chatty teenagers and dotty pensioners; where everyone gathers, no matter their age or economic status. With limited accommodation space it's no wonder the streets become communal property, and the perfect setting for both eating and socializing.

DAI PAI DONGS, AN ENDANGERED EATERY AT THE HEART OF HONG KONG CUISINE

One of the most memorable experiences during the trip was a visit to a *dai pai dong* to get a sense of the food, the atmosphere, the octopus-like dancing chef at the helm, and to watch the thrill, sense of accomplishment, tribute and adrenaline rush Jeremy had while first butchering and prepping crab with ginger and spring onions (recipe in this book).

The experience felt as though it was the culmination point of street food culture, community and culinary excellence, and as though we had been initiated into the true heart and essence of Hong Kong culture.

Tall bottles of cold beer divvied up into a four-finger pour among a table full of friends, set with a big stack of bowls, cups, chopsticks and spoons and a tub of boiling water, all to be washed by customers while waiting for the wok master to perform his duties. One by one the dishes come out when ready: steamed,